Health Care Nation

Whether a patient, health consumer, physician, nurse, health executive, or elected official, somewhere deep in our brains is this simple truth: the American health system isn't working, and it will only get worse if we don't do something about it.

Despite spending more money per capita on health care than any other country in the world, the United States struggles to match other nations in life expectancy, health outcomes, and general well-being. Meanwhile, the system spends more on unnecessary, ineffective, and wasteful services than what we collectively invest in K–12 education in America. All the while, our health status is declining.

This is a book about the interconnectedness between the health of people and the health of a nation. It's about the opportunity and responsibility each of us has to reimagine and reengineer a system that focuses on keeping all citizens healthy and caring for them when they are not.

We can and must take back the right we all have to be in better control of things that impact our health and well-being. This book awakens readers to the possibilities that exist today that are right in front of us if only we choose to see them.

This book is for those who want to change American health care from what it is to what *they believe it should be.*

"Tom Lawry does more than write about fixing health care—he rallies us to become the 'Rosa Parks of the system' to spark a movement of meaningful change. In this thought-provoking book, he offers a much-welcomed departure from the tireless blame game and fruitless top-down prescriptions that dominate health care reform discussions. Lawry hands the power back to us—patients, clinicians, business leaders, and advocates—showing how small, deliberate action can add up to transformative change."
Gil Bashe, *Chair, Global Health and Purpose, FINN Partners, Editor-in-Chief, Medika Life*

"Physicians and patients alike find themselves at the intersection of innovation and inequity in America's complex health care landscape. *Health Care Nation* serves as a timely and empowering call to action for those determined to restore purpose and integrity to a fractured system. Offering fresh perspectives and a focus on impactful solutions, this book inspires readers to take the lead in shaping a more equitable and effective future for health care."
Michael Suk, MD, JD, MPH, MBA, FACS, FACHE, *Chair, American Medical Association Board of Trustees*

"Growing up in the Black Belt of Alabama, I often heard my Aunt Molly say, 'If you have your health, you have everything.' This personal reflection underscores this book's profound assertion that health is foundational to a thriving society.

Health Care Nation delivers an urgent and compelling message about the state of health and healthcare in the United States. It boldly confronts the complex history of American healthcare and unveils the systemic design flaws that lead to its current inefficiencies, inequalities, and inequities.

This book is more than a call to action. It is a demand for transformative change."
Ronald Wyatt, MD, MHA, *Senior Fellow IHI, Founder and CEO, Achieving Health Equity LLC*

"The future is already here, but it is unevenly distributed. Tom Lawry is a modern-day health care soothsayer who sees this uneven distribution and has a clear-eyed vision to fix what is broken from the ground up. His plans are spot on, and if we grasp them now, we can make the changes we all seek. The question remains, however, are we listening closely to what he has to say? I know I am!"
David B. Nash, MD, MBA, *Founding Dean Emeritus, Jefferson College of Population Health*

"In his latest book, *Health Care Nation*, Tom Lawry envisions a future that prioritizes health, well-being, and equity for all citizens. This thought-provoking and insightful read challenges each of us to rethink the current system and take meaningful actions toward a more inclusive, efficient, and innovative health care future.

As a nurse, I have recognized the brokenness of US health-care and have always wanted to make it better. *Health Care Nation* is a manifesto for change that emphasizes the power of individual actions and innovative thinking in driving systemic change."
Kathleen McGrow, DNP, MS, RN, PMP, FHIMSS, FAAN, *Global Chief Nursing Innovation Officer, Microsoft*

"If you're motivated to change the healthcare system, then Tom Lawry's *Health Care Nation* equips you to do just that. The knowledge gained from *Health Care Nation* informs thinking and enables effective collaboration with others to bring about the change our nation needs. *Health Care Nation* is a must read for those who want to engage and looking for ways to begin or accelerate their work with others."
Ann Mond Johnson, *CEO, American Telemedicine Association*

Health Care Nation
The Future Is Calling and It's Better Than You Think

Tom Lawry

A PRODUCTIVITY PRESS BOOK

First published 2025
by Routledge
605 Third Avenue, New York, NY 10158

and by Routledge
4 Park Square, Milton Park, Abingdon, Oxon, OX14 4RN

Routledge is an imprint of the Taylor & Francis Group, an informa business

ISBN: 978-1-032-98802-3 (hbk)
ISBN: 978-1-032-96167-5 (pbk)
ISBN: 978-1-003-60069-5 (ebk)

DOI: 10.4324/9781003600695

This book is dedicated to those who believe health care is a noble cause and strive to make it so.

Contents

Foreword

Polly Greenberg Sarasohn, my mother, was President of the Health Council in our school district in suburban Detroit. Polly led her team of community business leaders, doctors, nurses, and educators, coming together to bring the polio vaccine to Francis Scott Key Elementary School in the Oak Park School District. The year: 1954.

My oldest sister Nancy, nine years my senior, received the Salk vaccine participating in the trial conducted among 623,972 school children from around the US sponsored by the National Foundation for Infantile Paralysis (aka March of Dimes). As one of the participants in the study, Nancy received an official "Polio Pioneer" pin.

Thanks to Nancy and the other Polio Pioneers, I remember standing in line in 1962 at Key Elementary School, receiving a sugar cube infused with the Sabin vaccine (channeling *Mary Poppins* which would become one of my favorite movies two years later – indeed, a spoonful of sugar helping that medicine go down!).

This is my first memory of being a health citizen: participating in a civic activity that benefited not only me as an individual but also my community of neighbors.

My mother worked at a job that had health insurance, and a generous plan at that: she belonged to a labor union and, living in Detroit in the 1960s, her health plan covered our entire family.

Eventually, she would count on that insurance to treat a tough case of lymphocytic leukemia. One facet of her therapy was to receive blood transfusions through the 1970s. And true to the definition of "union," her sisters and brothers in that organization participated in blood drives as a call-to-action for their fellow working member....another demonstration of health citizenship.

Every day, we make choices to engage in our health citizenship, from cooking and serving healthy food to quitting tobacco, participating in decision-making with our physicians, crowdsourcing our health data with other patients to drive toward cures, and even making TikTok videos sharing our experiences in battling cancer or depression.

When nurses and doctors support patients' voting in elections, that bolsters civic engagement in health care. When hospitals and health insurance plans enable price transparency for patients to understand their financial obligations for care and medicines, that helps support peoples' health and financial literacy. When technology is designed with users in mind – whether for patients' and caregivers' life-flows or for clinicians' workflows – health care gets better, enabling both the nurse and doctor and their patient to spend time in care and counsel – not clerical work that's spirit-zapping.

If you know Tom Lawry through his pioneering work in AI and health care, you only know part of his origin story inspiring him to write this book. Tom spent the first years of his career working in hospitals and health systems, affording him an ecosystem-wide view on the U.S. Health Care Nation as one of millions in the American health care workforce. Health care also happens to be the largest (and among fastest-growing) single sector of workers in the US, numbering 22 million people.

In *Health Care Nation*, the book, Tom asks us to consider many questions about health care in America. He doesn't prescribe "the" solution, but asks us to examine our lives and work, our experiences with providers and payers and pharma and all the touchpoints that have formed our collective view that health care in America is, in a word, broken....and breaking our household and national economies.

The solutions, plural, are in our hands, he asserts: in our daily decisions, and in the voting booth where, if our eyes and hearts are open, we can see health baked into most public policies on the ballot, or implicit in the values of those for whom we cast our votes.

Welcome to *Health Care Nation* – where we can exercise our health citizenship one person at a time, one day at a time. And if we do so in sufficient numbers, then we may well have that better health care future Tom challenges us to envision.

Jane Sarasohn-Kahn
Health Economist, Advisor, Trend Weaver
Health Populi Blog and THINK-Health
November 2024

Preface

Unrest (Noun)

"a state of dissatisfaction, disturbance, and agitation in a group of people."

My editor suggested that this was not the best opening paragraph to use when trying to convince you to buy this book. Nevertheless, when I think about the imperative we have to fix health care, I wonder what Rosa Parks had for breakfast on the day she made history.

I mean, did she start her day like any other over a bowl of cereal thinking it was just another day? Or was she contemplating something bigger as she stared into her coffee cup that morning?

In the end, the details of her breakfast don't matter. What matters is that she'd had enough. Enough of a system that diminished her, enough of rules that kept her in her "place."

Her small but radical refusal to give up her seat sparked a movement that would change the course of history, culminating in the Civil Rights Act of 1964.

In writing this book, I find myself wondering: where is the Rosa Parks moment for health care?

The Health Care Crisis

Like civil rights in the 1960s, health care today is one of the defining social and economic issues of our time. You don't need a book to tell you that the American health care system is broken. You see it every day—in rising costs, declining health status, and the burnout of the very people who keep the system running.

And yet, we often approach changing health care as if it's someone else's job. We assume that the solution will come from policymakers, executives, or technology. But history tells us a different story. Change rarely comes from the top down. It starts with ordinary people taking small, meaningful actions.

This Book Is Different

Most books about health care reform do two things you will not find in this book. The first is to spend hundreds of pages assigning blame: insurance companies, hospital executives, pharmaceutical firms, government regulators—the list is endless.

The second thing most books on this topic do is serve as a platform for an author or organization to prescriptively *tell you their* view on how to "fix" the system.

This book is different. It doesn't assign blame because the system's dysfunction isn't the fault of a single group or institution. Instead, it's the result of deeply embedded flaws such as financial incentives and workflows that shape how we view, deliver, and pay for health care.

Blame won't fix that. Understanding will.

And while I have my views on changing health care, you won't find my prescription for fixing health care in the pages of this book.

This is not a book about telling you what to think. It's about helping you gain a better understanding of the underlying issues. More importantly, it's about helping *you discover or refine your own voice in keeping with your unique needs, values, and experiences.*

It's about you—and every reader—realizing that your views and voice matter. They are the starting point for real change.

A Revolution Hidden in Plain Sight

This book is for those who want to change American health care from what it is to what *they believe it should be.*

It's built on the idea that each of us has the power to take small, meaningful actions to transform health care. It emphasizes that creating change in the system isn't a matter of *talking* but a matter of *doing.*

Which is where you come in.

Health care won't fix itself. And it won't be fixed by the people comfortable with the status quo. But it *can* be changed by individuals like you—patients, clinicians, business leaders, and ordinary citizens—who refuse to accept the way things are and start imagining what they could be.

This book is for everyone whose life has been touched by the health care system. It's for:

- Patients frustrated by high costs and long waits,
- Consumers who envision a system that goes beyond pills and procedures to keep us healthy,
- Clinicians exhausted by burnout,
- Business owners struggling to provide health benefits,
- Provider and payer leaders working to make sense of an impossibly complex system,
- The un- or underinsured who are one step away from bankruptcy if they get sick.

Like Rosa Parks, within each of us is a spark of an idea to make our lives and the lives of others better. This book is about ordinary people taking small actions that collectively lead to the next social revolution.

Each of us has the power to say "enough." And when enough of us do, the system will have no choice but to change.

T.

Author

Tom Lawry is a leading transformation advisor to health and medical leaders around the world, a top keynote speaker, and the best-selling author of *Hacking Healthcare—How AI and the Intelligent Health Revolution Will Reboot an Ailing System*.

He's the Managing Director of Second Century Tech and a former Microsoft executive who served as National Director for AI for Health and Life Sciences, Director of Worldwide Health, and Director of Organizational Performance for the company's first health incubator.

Prior to Microsoft, Tom was a Senior Director at GE Healthcare, the founder of two venture-backed health care software companies, a health system executive, and a hospital board member.

Tom's work and views have been featured in *Forbes, CEO Magazine, Harvard Business Review*, CNET, *Inside Precision Medicine*, and numerous webcasts and podcasts.

In a Harris Poll, Tom was named one of the most recognized leaders driving change and engagement in health care today. He has also been named one of the Top 20 '24 Voices to Follow in AI and Digital by Medika.

AWARENESS

We are not powerless unless we choose to be.

Scan me!

Scan this code for a message from the Author

Chapter 1

100 Billion and Counting

"Change will not come if we wait for some other person or some other time. We are the ones we've been waiting for. We are the change that we seek."

—*Barack Obama*

Congratulations to all of us! For the first time ever, there are now more than 8 billion humans alive and roaming the planet we call Earth. Look out Mars, we're coming for you next! Ever since we developed opposable digits and began walking upright, there have only been a total of 100 billion humans.[1]

Imagine that.

And despite future pandemics, other forces of nature, and our own self-inflicted disasters, the human race is expected to see a dramatic increase in both numbers and how long we live.[2] As you let this sink in, here is an important question to consider:

What responsibility do we have to ourselves and the next 100 billion humans coming onto the planet Earth?

DOI: 10.4324/9781003600695-2

No matter what generational tribe you belong to, this is the *"holy grail"* of questions. It's at the heart of everything from why you think we exist to what moves you believe should be made to reimagine our approach to health, well-being, and happiness for ourselves and others.

How we answer this question is the ultimate inheritance we can provide to our fellow homo sapiens and the planet. Believe it or not, it's also something *each of us* has the power to influence and direct.

Whether you're driven by a personal desire to live a long, healthy, and happy life, or by a sense of responsibility to protect our planet for the future of our children, grandchildren, and others, the choices we make today will have lasting effects on the generations to come.

The Starting Point for All Things Is Health

What is your vision for leading a great life? What dreams do you have for your family and loved ones? What should we do to make the world better? Whatever the movie that plays in your head looks like, it is in some way anchored to health, well-being, and happiness.

And while good health is important to everyone on the planet, it's the number one goal among Americans.[3] All other goals like financial and career success are a distant second. These are also highly dependent on health.[4]

In pursuit of this goal, Americans invest more than any other country in our quest for health. Every year we dig into our pockets and spend hundreds of billions of dollars on fitness memberships, gym equipment, organic foods, dietary supplements, health apps, medical services, and wellness retreats, among other things. This figure has steadily increased over the years as people become more health-conscious and seek ways to improve their well-being.

But by far the largest investment we make as individuals and a nation is in the U.S. health care system. You contribute to it every time you get a paycheck, pay your taxes or insurance premiums, pony up for a medical co-pay or deductible, or buy an American-made product.

In exchange for these investments, we've created the most technologically sophisticated medical complex the world has ever seen. We staff it with the best medical experts. The system does *AMAZING things*.

But here's the problem: Most of these *AMAZING things* aren't very relevant to your health, well-being, or happiness.

Whether a patient, health consumer, physician, nurse, health executive, or elected official, somewhere deep in many of our brains is this simple truth: the current health system isn't working, and it will only get worse if we don't do something about it.

Today the US spends more on health care per capita than any other country, and yet it lags behind in life expectancy, health outcomes, and overall well-being.[5] Meanwhile, the system burns through more money on unnecessary and wasteful services than what we collectively invest in the K-12 education of our children.[6]

All the while, our health status is declining. For the first time, kids born today may not live as long as their older siblings.

If you are reading this, you are either concerned or curious about the current situation and what can be done to change course.

The Waiting Is Over

We keep waiting for someone to come along and fix America's health problem. And that *is* the problem. Waiting for someone else to come along and fix things hasn't worked. There is no one else. There is only us.

This is a book about the interconnectedness between the health of people and the health of a nation. It's about the opportunity and responsibility each of us has to reimagine and reengineer a system that focuses on keeping *all* citizens healthy and *caring for them* when they are not.

We can and must take back the right we all have to be in better control of things that impact our health and well-being. It's an awakening to the possibilities that exist today that are right in front of us if only we choose to see them.

Believe it or not, there's a role you can play and actions you can take to determine the health and economic well-being of your children's, children's children. It's about understanding. It's about finding and using your voice to drive positive change.

Just as you hold this book in your hands, so too do you hold the power to change the system. Within each of us are the seeds of a new order of things.

You are here. The time *is now*. *We* are the ones.

If you are curious about the possibilities, then turn the page. I'd like to explain why the past approaches to fixing health care have failed.

For Your Consideration:

1. Do you believe that America's health care system needs to be fixed? What parts do you see working versus what parts are not?
2. How do you see the current health care in America impacting you, your family, and society?
3. Is health care a social justice issue? How does it compare to the other issues important to you?
4. Have you or someone close to you had an experience with the health care system that influences your views?
5. Do you believe that there are actions you can take to make a difference in changing how health care works? Why or why not?

Notes:

Endnotes

1. World Population Prospects, 2022, United Nations Department of Economic and Social Affairs, 2022 https://www.un.org/development/desa/pd/sites/www.un.org.development.desa.pd/files/wpp2022_summary_of_results.pdf
2. World Population Prospects, 2022, United Nations Department of Economic and Social Affairs, 2022 https://www.un.org/development/desa/pd/sites/www.un.org.development.desa.pd/files/wpp2022_summary_of_results.pdf
3. Lydia Saad, Seven in 10 Americans Likely to Set Goals for 2023, Gallup, January 5, 2023, https://news.gallup.com/poll/467696/seven-americans-likely-set-goals-2023.aspx
4. Lydia Saad, Seven in 10 Americans Likely to Set Goals for 2023, Gallup, January 5, 2023, https://news.gallup.com/poll/467696/seven-americans-likely-set-goals-2023.aspx
5. Jamie Duchard, Exclusive: More Than 70% of Americans Feel Failed by the Health Care System, Time, May 16, 2023, https://time.com/6279937/us-health-care-system-attitudes/
6. How Does the U.S. Healthcare System Compare to Other Countries? Peter G. Peterson Foundation, August 15, 2023, https://www.pgpf.org/blog/2023/07/how-does-the-us-healthcare-system-compare-to-other-countries

Chapter 2

America's Largest Escape Room

"All great changes are preceded by chaos."

—*Deepak Chopra*

Escape rooms have become quite popular these days. This is a game where people are locked in a room and must work as a team to discover clues, solve puzzles, and accomplish a series of tasks to escape.

In many ways, today's health care system is America's largest escape room. We've locked our most talented health experts and consumers in a labyrinth along with a staggering $4.7 trillion of our own money.[1]

The problem is that we haven't figured out how to escape the maze of convoluted policies, skewed financial incentives, and entrenched traditions that are steering amazing people and 17.6% of our Gross Domestic Production (GDP) in the wrong direction.[2]

Despite these flaws, it's important to recognize that the United States is a global leader in scientific discovery and developing innovative technologies to diagnose and treat

DOI: 10.4324/9781003600695-3

disease. It's also important to understand that health professionals, provider organizations, health insurance plans, and other diverse entities are doing their best to bring those advancements forward.

But here is the rub—the hodgepodge that we call the American health care system emerged at different points in our nation's history, under varied contexts, and for very different purposes. *This mishmash of systems was never designed to function as a single, coherent system.*

The renowned newscaster Walter Cronkite nailed it years ago when he quipped that our health care system is *"neither healthy, caring, nor a system."*

Whether you're a Medicare recipient or a health professional, we're all stuck in the same quandary. We tell ourselves we can and must do better. We just don't know where to start.

I landed my first job as a junior executive in a major medical center when I was 24 years old. Since then, I've spent my career in and around health care in America, Europe, and Asia. Whether a neurosurgeon in Charlotte or an herbalist in China, I've never met anyone in health care who didn't have good intentions. Everyone wants to be part of a noble cause. They're in it for the greater good—to foster better health and a better world.

Unfortunately, the complexities of America's health care juggernaut have a knack for leading even the smartest, most well-intentioned people and mission-driven organizations astray. It's a collective conundrum. *It's no one's fault and everyone's fault.* And therein lies the crux of the problem: no single entity can shoulder the burden of fixing health care. *It's a shared responsibility.*

This is one of the reasons we feel helpless to change it. It's also why we keep getting the narrative wrong on how to "fix" health care. This path typically plays out in one of two ways.

The Blame Game

In the grand theater of health care reform, we've long played the *blame game*. It's where we pass the mantle of villainy from one scapegoat to another. Today, it's "Big Pharma" under the spotlight in the U.S. Senate. Tomorrow it might be the payers or the health providers. It's a well-rehearsed drama, with elected leaders grilling health execs for the cameras, generating headlines and sound bites for the folks back home.

But for all its flair, this blame game is just that—a game. It's a distraction, a sideshow that fails to illuminate the real issues at the heart of our ailing health care system.

Let's agree that exorbitant drug prices, incomprehensible benefit statements, and bloated administrative costs are big problems. Let us also understand that these are glaring symptoms of a much deeper malady.

Just as treating symptoms without dealing with the underlying cause won't solve a medical problem, pointing fingers at one group or another, including elected leaders, only serves to obscure the true diagnosis of what's wrong with health care and what needs to change.

We're all stuck in an escape room of our own making. Good people are trapped in a system devoid of coherence and cooperation.

The tangled web of incentives and disjointed coordination among players in the health care delivery system leads to a nonsensical allocation of resources. Quality suffers, costs soar, outcomes falter, and patients are left navigating a maze of frustration.

Railing against the system won't untangle these knots. Changing the system starts with changing the narrative.

Let's shift the focus from blame to understanding.

Let's dispense with the notion of *"bad players."* Instead, let's shine a light on the flawed processes and misaligned incentives driving a dysfunctional behemoth that is impacting our health, wallets, and the strength of a nation.

We won't fix what's broken by bashing it. What we need is a collective vision, a shared understanding of the current forces at play, and a commitment to steer health care in the right direction.

Understanding what's driving today's system is no easy feat. Another step in grasping the intricacies of our health care conundrum is to stop asking the wrong questions and start asking the right ones.

The Wrong Question: How Much Can We Save?

Health policy or reform discussions often focus on how changing our approach to health care will *"save money."* Whether it's about saving or spending, the fixation on financial outcomes misses the point entirely.

Prevention, for instance, shouldn't be judged solely on its ability to pinch pennies. It's about investing in the well-being of our society, not just balancing the books. It's about the *value* we all get from the investment we're making.

A paradigm shift is imperative, one that elevates things like prevention to its rightful stature alongside diagnostics and treatment. We must scrutinize every facet of health care through the lens of *value maximization*.

Does an intervention enhance health outcomes? Are there alternatives that yield comparable or better results at a lower cost?

Evidence speaks volumes. Effective preventive measures, both clinical and communal, stand ready to alleviate the burden of chronic ailments, safeguarding both present and future generations. The toll exacted by preventable diseases, both human and economic, serves as a stark reminder of why change is needed now.

It's time we chart a new course for health care that prioritizes long-term prosperity over short-sighted austerity.

So, let's change the script. Let's stop chasing shadows and start shedding light on the real issues. Let's ask the right questions and, more importantly, let's find the answers together. That's the only way we'll break free from the blame game and build a health care system worthy of the name.

By now you are probably wondering whether change is possible and asking yourself whether you have the power to change anything. If I'm correct turn the page. There is something I'd like you to know about how and why we disempower ourselves.

For Your Consideration:

1. This chapter suggests that good people are trapped in flawed system. Do you agree?
2. Do you think that making health care better is a shared responsibility or should some groups bear more accountability than others when it comes to fixing issues with the current system?
3. What are the most pressing issues facing the health care system today? Do these issues impact you or your loved ones personally?
4. Do you believe the current health care system provides good value for the money we invest? Why or why not?
5. What is the most significant barrier to achieving a more coherent and effective health care system? Is it the system's complexity, financial interests, political challenges, or something else?

Notes:

_____

_____

_____

_____

_____

_____

_____

_____

_____

_____

_____

_____

Endnotes

1. National Health Expenditures 2022 Highlights, CMS, December 13, 2023, https://www.cms.gov/newsroom/fact-sheets/national-health-expenditures-2022-highlights
2. National Health Expenditures 2022 Highlights, CMS, December 13, 2023, https://www.cms.gov/newsroom/fact-sheets/national-health-expenditures-2022-highlights

Chapter 3

Changing Health Care Starts with Changing Our Minds

"All things are ready, if our mind be so."
—*William Shakespeare*

Changing the system starts with finding a cure for an affliction infecting caregivers, leaders, and citizens alike. There is no magic pill or miracle cure for this malady. It's a condition of the spirit I call *health care fatalism*.

Health care fatalism is a condition marked by a creeping sense of unrest and discontent with a system that isn't working. Symptoms include feelings of anger, despair and hopelessness. It often includes a sense of resignation that we don't have the power to alter the course of what is happening, which leads us to believe that there is no point in personally trying to change anything.

Start your journey by assessing whether you are suffering from a case of health care fatalism. Understand that such thoughts limit your potential to dream and advocate for a

 DOI: 10.4324/9781003600695-4

better system. This keeps you from taking action and having impact.

Whether you are a single parent frightened and confused by today's system, a nurse walking out the door to cover your shift at a regional medical center, or a small business owner meeting your insurance broker, this question is the starting point.

We all get to choose our frame of mind which leads to feeling empowered or disempowered.

Hope as the Antidote

Did you know that hope is more than an emotion? It's a cognitive behavioral process used by people daily to create a pathway to achieving a goal.

Believe it or not, there is an emerging science around understanding and leveraging hope to help solve societal issues.

Researchers at the University of Oklahoma's Hope Research Center define hope as *"the belief that the future will be better and you have the power to make it so. Hope is based on three main ideas: desirable goals, pathways to goal attainment, and agency (willpower) to pursue those pathways."*[1]

Hope isn't a denial of what is, but a belief that the current situation is not all that can be. It's the recognition that something's wrong, but also that it's not the end of the story.[2]

Unlike optimism, which is simply the expectation of a better future, hope is action-oriented and a skill that can be learned.

Reaping the benefits of hope involves reframing thoughts and forming new habits. But with a shift to your mindset and habits, you can begin to see and work toward the possibility of a better future—and equip others to do the same.

Each of us has the ability to articulate a view or take actions that, no matter how small, build momentum for change. A simple step is to begin micro-dosing hope. More on the power of small actions is given in Chapter 16.

Another factor that keeps us from acting is the sheer complexity of the system itself.

Think about it: If the health care system wasn't as complicated as it is, would we allow it to exist as it is? The complexity of today's health system is disguising what is happening to our money and our right to better health.

It's hard to change something you don't understand. If you are curious to learn more then turn the page. I'd like to explain the paradox of the American health care system.

For Your Consideration:

1. Do you agree with the concept of "health care fatalism" described in the chapter?
2. The chapter suggests that changing our mindset is the first step to changing the health care system. What are some thoughts or beliefs you hold about health care that might need to change to empower *you* to take action?
3. Consider your own experiences with the health care system. Do you find it overly complex and confusing?
4. What do you think about the concept of hope being the starting point for change?
5. If you were to educate others about the challenges of health care how would you encourage others to adopt a mindset that includes hope and empowers change?

Notes:

_____

_____

_____

_____

_____

_____

_____

_____

_____

_____

_____

_____

_____

_____

Endnotes

1. Hope Research Center, University of Oklahoma, https://www.ou.edu/tulsa/hope
2. Ashley Abramson, Hope as the antidote, American Psychological Association, January 1, 2024, https://www.apa.org/monitor/2024/01/trends-hope-greater-meaning-life

Chapter 4

America's Health Paradox

Here is something that many health care leaders are fond of saying:

"The American Health care System is the best in the world!"

In some respects, this statement is true.

If you are going to get sick and have great insurance or lots of money, there is no better place to do so than in the United States. We excel at taking care of *really sick* people.

Medical miracles are performed daily by an amazing cadre of clinicians who have access to the best technology, facilities, and pharmaceuticals.

In this regard, we are the envy of the rest of the world.

And why shouldn't Americans have the best of everything? After all, we are the world's leader in health care spending. This includes per capita spending and the percentage of the national income spent on health care.

 DOI: 10.4324/9781003600695-5

As of this writing, America spends an average of $14,570 per citizen for a total of $4.7 trillion a year.[1]

Here's what $4.7 trillion looks like:

$4,700,000,000,000

America's health spending is two to three times more than other high-income nations like the UK, Canada, Germany, Japan, and Australia, where health coverage is universal (Figure 4.1).

Where does all this money come from? Mainly from you and your employer in the form of taxes, health insurance premiums, and the out-of-pocket expenses you pay whenever encountering today's health system. It's also a hidden cost that is built into the products and services produced by any American company that provides health benefits.

United States	$12,555
Switzerland	$8,049
Germany	$8,011
Austria	$7,275
Netherlands	$6,729
Comparable Country Average	$6,651
France	$6,630
Belgium	$6,600
Sweden	$6,438
Australia	$6,372
Canada	$6,319
Uniter Kingdom	$5,493
Japan	$5,251

Figure 4.1   Health Expenditures Per Capita, U.S. Dollars, 2022.

Source: KFF analysis of OECD data Get the data PNG.

One in eight jobs in America is in health care.[2] Nearly one-fifth of the U.S. economy goes to paying for health care. And yet, despite our inventiveness and massive expenditures, the delivery of care and outcomes are wildly uneven.

Health care in America today is a patchwork of disparity.

The richest men in America live longer than the average man in any country (Figure 4.2). The poorest have life expectancies comparable to men in Sudan and Pakistan.[3]

Even with all our wealth, Americans are among the least healthy people in the rich world, and among the most likely to die early.

If you are reading this as a resident of Mississippi, you probably won't live as long as someone from Bangladesh (Figure 4.3).[4,5,6]

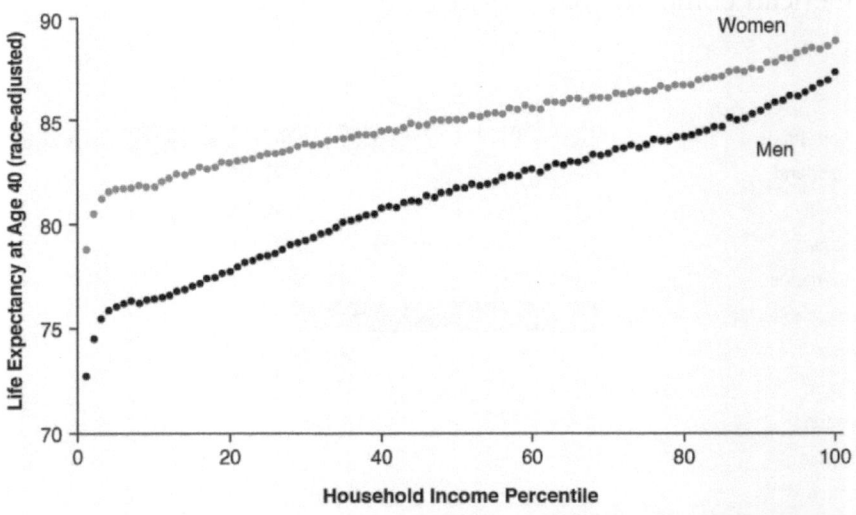

Figure 4.2   Life Expectancy vs Income in the US.

Source: Boston University School of Public Health

Notes: The richest American men live 15 years longer than the poorest men, while the richest American women live 10 years longer than the poorest women.

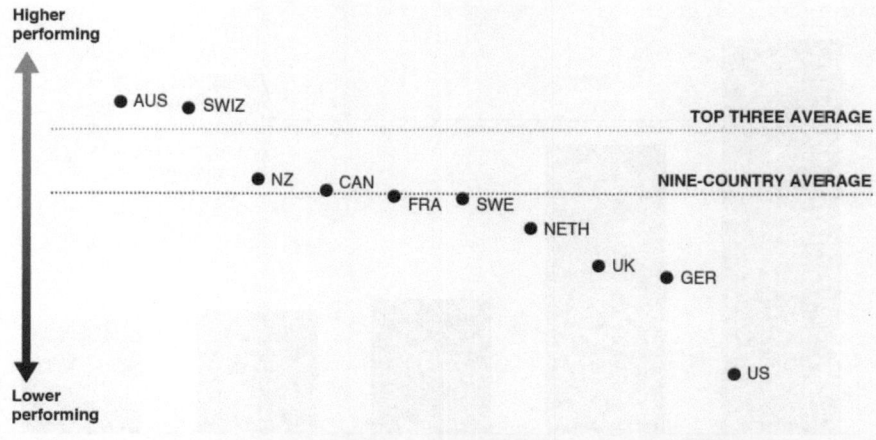

Figure 4.3 Americans Live the Shortest Lives and Have the Most Avoidable Deaths.

Data: Commonwealth Fund analysis.

Maternal mortality rates for American women are worse than most third-world countries. Even more unexplainable is that Black women are *three times more likely to die* of childbirth than White women. This gap is worse today than it was when we began keeping records in the early 1900's—which was not a time considered to be a high point in history for woman or Black Americans (Figure 4.4).[7]

Drugs and alcohol abuse continue harming Americans in record numbers. Ninety-four percent of those with substance-use disorders do not get treatment, even though this pays for itself many times over.[8],[9]

The US is a global leader in *avoidable amputations*. Think about that...*AVOIDABLE* amputations. This is mainly due to inconsistencies in how we manage diabetes which impacts 38.4 million Americans, or almost 12 percent of the population.[10]

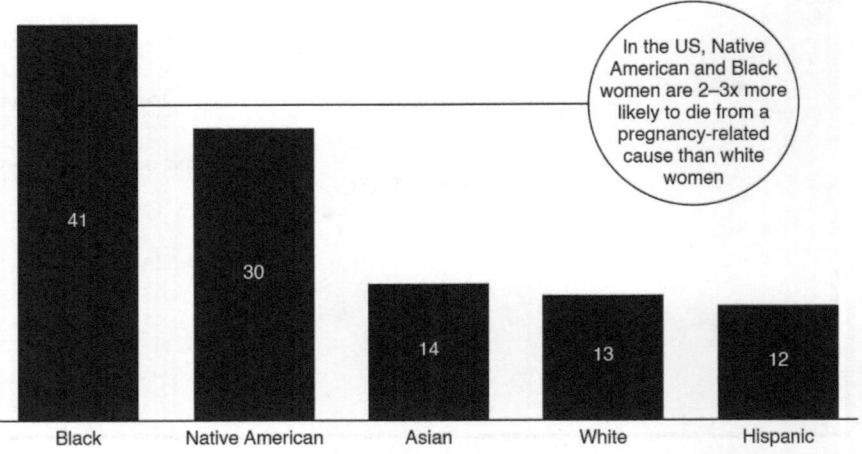

In the US, Native American and Black women are 2–3x more likely to die from a pregnancy-related cause than white women

41

30

14

13

12

Black | Native American | Asian | White | Hispanic

Figure 4.4 Disparities Across Ethnicities in Maternal Deaths in the US.

Sources: James, A.H., Federspiel, J.J. and Ahmadzia, H.K., "Desparities in Obstetrics Hemorrhage Outcomes"; U.S. Centers for Disease Control and Prevention, "Racial/Ethnic Disparities in Pregnancy-Related Deaths – United States, 2007–2016".

And speaking of avoidable, 30 million Americans die prematurely each year from *preventable diseases*. Twenty-seven percent of U.S. health-care spending goes to managing health and medical conditions *that are preventable*.[11]

Wrap your mind around that for a moment. Think about friends and family members who have been impacted. Many of the chronic conditions that have taken our loved ones are reversible if caught early (Figure 4.5).[12] Beyond the premature loss of life, these conditions alone have a combined economic burden of $590 billion a year.[13]

Looking at how the system works (or doesn't work) makes one wonder whether these stark inequities are driven by cost considerations or indifference.

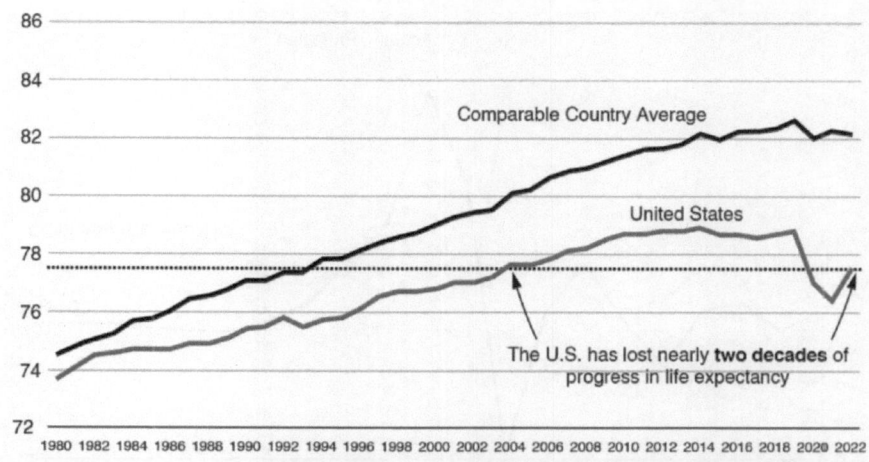

Figure 4.5   Life Expectancy, at Birth, in Years—1980–2022.

Source: KFF analysis of CDC, OECD, Australian Bureau of Statistics, Japanese Ministry of Health, Labour, and Welfare, Statistics Canada, and the UK. Office for National Statistics data Get the data PNG.

If nothing changes, the cost of supporting the current system will continue to grow faster than the economy with little hope of seeing better outcomes (Figure 4.6).[14]

Now, imagine a new paradigm. It's a system that produces *"health dividends"* that are seen by preventing diseases and health conditions that currently consume more than a quarter of our health resources. More on the health dividend concept in Chapter 14.

Turn the page to learn more about how the American Health care System stacks up against the performance of other countries in creating health for its citizens.

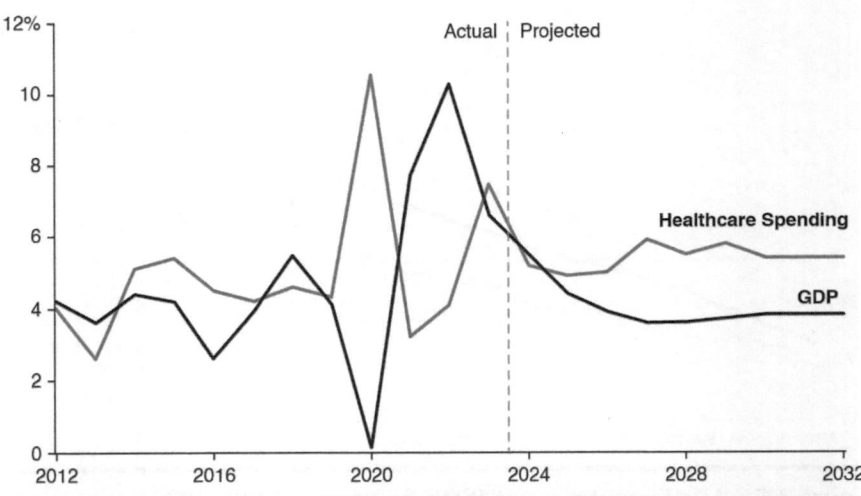

Figure 4.6   Health Care Spending Is Projected to Grow Faster than the Economy.

Sources: Congressional Budget Office, Office of Management and Budget, Centers for Medicare and Medicaid Services, Peter G. Peterson Foundation.

For Your Consideration:

1. Do you believe that the American Health care System is the *"best in the world"*? Why or why not?
2. What thoughts or emotions do the health disparities described in this chapter evoke in you? Why do you think such disparities exist?
3. What are your thoughts on the relationship between social justice and health care?

Notes:

Endnotes

1. Anne B. Martin, Micah Hartman, Benjamin Washington, Aaron Catlin, National Health Expenditures In 2023: Faster Growth As Insurance Coverage And Utilization Increased, Health Affairs, December 18, 2024, https://www.healthaffairs.org/doi/10.1377/hlthaff.2024.01375
2. Derek Thomson, Health Care Just Became the U.S.'s Largest Employer. *The Atlantic*, 2018, https://www.theatlantic.com/business/archive/2018/01/health-care-america-jobs/550079/
3. Raj Chetty, Michael Stepner, Sarah Abraham, Shelby Lin, Benjamin Scuderi, Nicholas Turner, Augustin Bergeron, and David Cutler, Income and Life Expectancy in the United States: Executive Summary, The Health Inequality Project, April 2016, https://www.healthinequality.org/documents/paper/healthineq_summary.pdf
4. Nicholas Kristof, How Do We Fix the Scandal That Is American Health Care? *New York Times*, https://www.nytimes.com/2023/08/16/opinion/health-care-life-expectancy-poverty.html?smid=em-share
5. Life Expectancy at Birth by State, National Center for Health Statistics, https://www.cdc.gov/nchs/pressroom/sosmap/life_expectancy/life_expectancy.htm (cdc.gov)
6. Life Expectancy at Birth – Bangladesh, World Bank Group, https://data.worldbank.org/indicator/SP.DYN.LE00.IN?locations=BD
7. Achievements in Public Health, 1900–1999: Healthier Mothers and Babies, Centers for Disease Control (CDC) (cdc.gov)
8. SAMHSA Announces National Survey on Drug Use and Health (NSDUH) Results Detailing Mental Illness and Substance Use Levels in 2021, U.S. Department of Health and Human Services' (HHS) Substance Abuse and Mental Health Services Administration (SAMHSA), January, 2023, https://www.hhs.gov/about/news/2023/01/04/samhsa-announces-national-survey-drug-use-health-results-detailing-mental-illness-substance-use-levels-2021.html#:~:text=In%202021%2C%2094%25%20of%20people,not%20think%20they%20needed%20treatment.
9. Susan L Ettner, David Huang, Elizabeth Evans, Danielle Rose Ash, Mary Hardy, and Yih-Ing Hser, Benefit–Cost in the California Treatment Outcome Project: Does Substance Abuse

Treatment "Pay for Itself"?, Hospital Research and Educational Trust/ Association for Health Services Research, February, 2006, https://www.ncbi.nlm.nih.gov/pmc/articles/PMC1681530/

10. Nicholas Kristof, How Do We Fix the Scandal That Is American Health Care? *New York Times*, https://www.nytimes.com/2023/08/16/opinion/health-care-life-expectancy-poverty.html?smid=em-share

11. Sandro Galea, and Nason Maani, The Cost of Preventable Disease in the US. *The Lancet*, October, 2020, https://www.thelancet.com/journals/lanpub/article/PIIS2468-2667(20)30204-8/fulltext

12. Sergey Young, The Science and Technology of Growing Young.

13. US Chronic Disease Management Growth, Frost & Sullivan, October 2021.

14. Healthcare Spending Will Be One Fifth of the Economy Within a Decade, Peter G Petersen Foundation, September 16, 2024.

Chapter 5

If Health Care Was a Sport, We Wouldn't Make the Playoffs

"Healthy citizens are the greatest asset any country can have."

—Winston Churchill

In the last chapter, we looked at the paradox of the current health system. It helps some but not all citizens maintain a degree of health and wellness. For others, it does little to help them be healthy, happy, or productive.

Let's open the performance lens a little wider. How does the U.S. health care system perform compared to the health systems of other countries?

The Commonwealth Fund is a private foundation started in 1918 by one of America's first female philanthropists, Anna Harkness. Its mission is to research and promote high-performing health care systems to achieve better access, improved quality, and greater efficiency, particularly for society's most vulnerable citizens.

DOI: 10.4324/9781003600695-6

	AUS	CAN	FRA	GER	NETH	NZ	SWE	SWIZ	UK	US
OVERALL RANKING	1	7	5	9	2	4	6	8	3	10
Access to Care	9	7	6	3	1	5	4	8	2	10
Care Process	5	4	7	9	3	1	10	6	8	2
Administrative Efficiency	2	5	4	8	6	3	7	10	1	9
Equity	1	7	6	2	3	8	–	4	5	9
Health Care Outcomes	1	4	5	9	7	3	6	2	8	10

Figure 5.1   Health care System Performance Rankings.

Source: David Blumenthal et al., Mirror, Mirror 2024: A Portrait of the Failing U.S. Health System – Comparing Performance In 10 Nations (Commonwealth Fund, Sept. 2024). https://dot.org/1D.26099naOg-2p66

According to data from the Commonwealth Fund, the U.S. health care system is the most expensive in the world. Despite our enormous investments, we are at the bottom of the list in overall health including access to care, administrative efficiency, equity, and health care outcomes (Figure 5.1).[1]

It's important to note that America's poor comparative performance is not an indictment of the talented, dedicated people who work in health, nor is it a reflection of the worthiness of the mission of health organizations or the science behind all of it.

So why is America first in spending but last in results? There are many factors impacting our performance that we'll go into in subsequent chapters. For now, many studies conclude that a causal factor is the reactive nature of the U.S. health system.

Characteristics of a reactive model include[2]:

- Many citizens have little or no access to health and medical services.
- Most health expenditures support a "break-fix" model of care delivery.
- Minimal investments are made in health improvements (as a percentage of total health care expenditures).

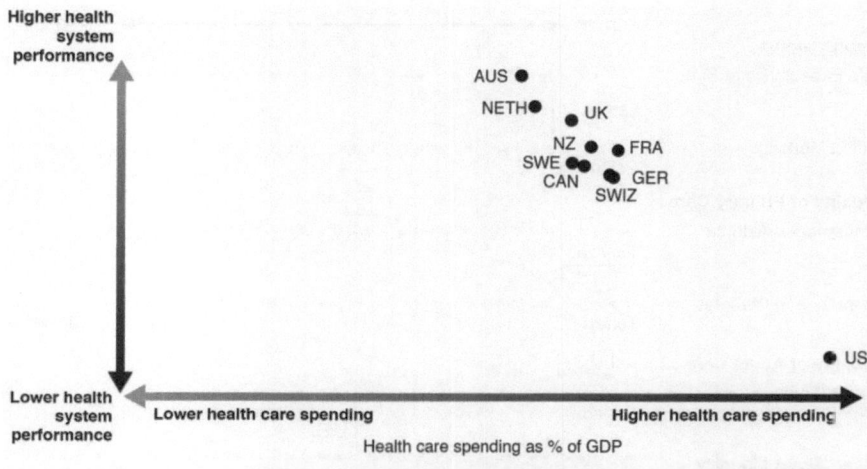

Figure 5.2 Health care System Performance Compared to Spending.

Source: Commonwealth Fund Analysis.

As a result of the characteristics noted above, U.S. spending on inpatient and outpatient care is about twice that of comparable countries.[3]

Another category where the US stands out is administrative spending. It's more than four times higher than other comparable countries. At last count, the U.S. health care system spends over $900 per person per year on administrative costs.[4]

Why is it so high? One of the reasons is the cost of maintaining a fragmented system. This is characterized by a patchwork of private insurers, providers and government rules and regulations. This exacerbates both inefficiencies and inequities.

An additional view to consider is the characteristics that the top-performing countries and health systems have in common. Traits that distinguish top-performing countries from the US include[5]:

■ All citizens have universal coverage for basic health services.

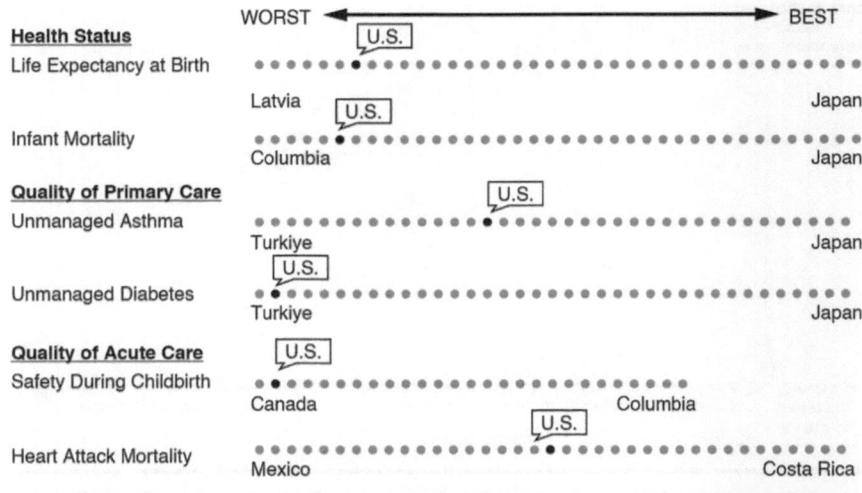

Figure 5.3 Although the US Spends More on Health Care than Other Developed Countries, Its Health Outcomes are Generally Not Any Better.

Source: Organisation for Economic Co-operation and Development, OECD Health Statistics 2023, July 2023.

- Cost barriers to accessing care are low or nonexistent
- Priority is given to investing in primary care systems to ensure that high-value services are equitably available in all communities to all people.
- Administrative burdens that divert time, efforts, and spending from health improvement efforts are low.
- Greater investments are made in social services, especially for children and working-age adults. They are considered part of the health care continuum.

Despite our high spending, the US is the only country among its peers that doesn't have universal health coverage. Within America, this topic is volatile and controversial. It's also the starting point for many of the performance issues we are seeing.

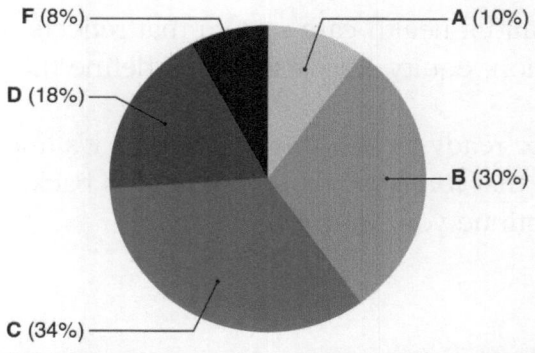

Figure 5.4   What Grade Would You Give the U.S. Healthcare System Overall?

Source: TIME-Harris Poll, https://time.com/6279937/us-health-care-system-attitudes/

Beyond global comparisons, more than 70% of U.S. adults feel the health care system is failing to meet their needs in at least one way, according to data from a Harris Poll (Figure 5.4).[6]

Changing the U.S. health care system is about understanding how to reinvest our economic and human resources to go from the bottom to the top of the list to become a global model for health and well-being. It's a path that going forward prioritizes prevention over treatment. Compassion over bureaucracy. A path that ensures that every citizen, regardless of income or background, has access to basic services and care they need which support living healthy and fulfilling lives.

Transformation will not come easy. It will require political will, institutional reform, and a collective commitment to the common good. It will require all of us *to challenge entrenched interests, confront systemic injustices, and reimagine a new future.*

Rising to this challenge means demanding better from our leaders, our institutions, and ourselves.

Let us build a health care system that reflects the values of compassion, equity, and justice that define the best of America.

If you are ready to join this movement, it's important to understand that *three key issues* holding us back. Turn the page to continue your journey.

For Your Consideration:

1. How do your experiences with the health system compare to the issues of access, equity, and efficiency discussed in the chapter?
2. The chapter highlights the absence of universal health coverage as a significant factor in the performance of America's health care system. What are your personal beliefs on universal health coverage? Do you think it should be implemented in the US? Why or why not?
3. Transformation of the health care system is described as requiring political will, institutional reform, and a collective commitment to the common good. In what ways do you feel empowered or disempowered to contribute to this transformation? What steps, however small, might you take to advocate for a more equitable and efficient health care system?

Notes:

_____

_____

_____

_____

_____

_____

_____

_____

_____

_____

_____

_____

_____

Endnotes

1. Mirror, Mirror 2024: A Portrait of the Failing U.S. Health System, Commonwealth Fund, September, 2023, https://www.commonwealthfund.org/publications/fund-reports/2024/sep/mirror-mirror-2024
2. Mirror, Mirror 2024: A Portrait of the Failing U.S. Health System, Commonwealth Fund, September, 2023, https://www.commonwealthfund.org/publications/fund-reports/2024/sep/mirror-mirror-2024
3. Li Lin. Mico Mrkaic, U.S. Healthcare: A Story of Rising Market Power, Barriers to Entry, and Supply Constraints. *IMF eLibrary*, July 6, 2021, https://www.elibrary.imf.org/configurable/content/journals$002f001$002f2021$002f180$002farticle-A001-en.xml?t:ac=journals%24002f001%24002f2021%24002f180%24002farticle-A001-en.xml
4. How Does the U.S. Healthcare System Compare to Other Countries? Peter G. Petersen Foundation, August 15, 2024, https://www.pgpf.org/blog/2024/08/how-does-the-us-healthcare-system-compare-to-other-countries.
5. Mirror, Mirror 2024: Reflecting Poorly, Commonwealth Fund, https://www.commonwealthfund.org/publications/fund-reports/2021/aug/mirror-mirror-2021-reflecting-poorly
6. Jamie Ducharme, Exclusive: More Than 70% of Americans Feel Failed by the Health Care System. Time, May 16, 2023, https://time.com/6279937/us-health-care-system-attitudes/

Chapter 6

Life, Liberty, and the Pursuit of a Low-Deductible Health Plan

Good health is the foundation of life, liberty, and happiness. Unfortunately, our nation's founders never got around to debating *life, liberty, and the pursuit of a low-deductible health plan*. As a result, *health care in the United States is not a right.*

There is no mention of it in the Constitution or Bill of Rights. Our forefathers didn't purposely excluded health care when they were defining inalienable rights. They simply had no concept of what was to come. When fundamental rights were being defined in the 1700s, the average life expectancy of an American was 35.[1] Medical treatments in colonial days often *reduced* life expectancy.

When health care is not a right, some people and populations have little or no access to health services. This makes them less likely to be healthy. This in turn creates a lifelong

 DOI: 10.4324/9781003600695-7

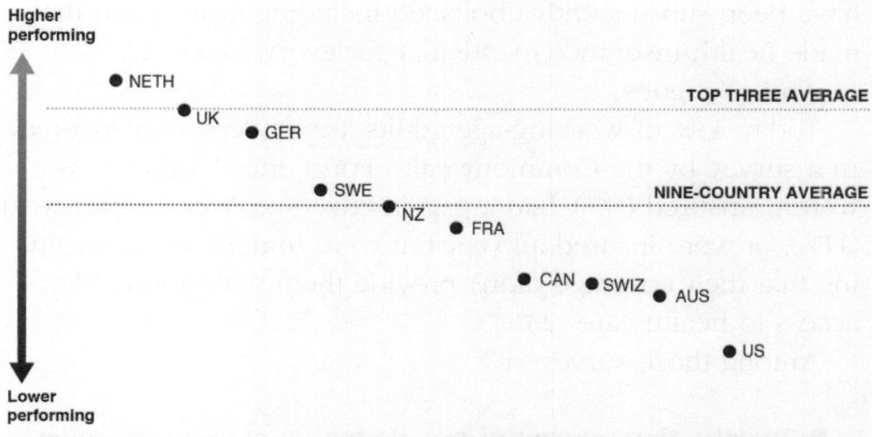

Figure 6.1 Americans Face the Most Barriers to Accessing and Affording Health Care.

Source: David Blumenthal et al., Mirror, Mirror 2024: A Portrait of the Failing U.S Health System-Comparing Performance in 10 Nations (Commonwealth Fund, Sept. 2024). https://doi.org/10.26099/ta0g-zp66

drag on things like education and career paths impacting their ability to pursue and achieve their full potential (Figure 6.1).

As a result of health not being a constitutionally guaranteed right, our citizen-elected leaders have not come to terms with legislation that makes health care a right or at least provides a pathway to universal access to a baseline of health and medical services for all citizens.

Many elected leaders have attempted to resolve this oversight. In the 1950's President Truman offered up a national health program to include all Americans. It was denounced by the American Medical Association (AMA) and called a communist plot by a Congressional House subcommittee.

In 2010 President Obama's efforts for universal access to health care led to the passage of the Affordable Care Act (ACA). And while parts of the ACA, colloquially known as Obamacare, are still in effect, many key components of the act have been subsequently abolished including a provision that made health insurance mandatory for every American.

And so it goes.

Today 43% of working-age adults are inadequately insured. In a survey by the Commonwealth Fund, these individuals were uninsured (9%), had a gap in coverage over the past year (11%), or were insured all year but were underinsured, meaning that their coverage didn't provide them with affordable access to health care (23%).[2]

Among those surveyed:

■ Twenty-nine percent of people with employer coverage and 44% of those with coverage purchased through the individual market and marketplaces were underinsured.
■ Forty-six percent had skipped or delayed care because of the cost, and 42% said they had problems paying medical bills or were paying off medical debt.
■ Half (49%) said they would be unable to pay for an unexpected $1,000 medical bill within 30 days, including 68% of adults with low income, 69% of Black adults, and 63% of Latinx/Hispanic adults.

Most of those who are uninsured or underinsured suffer significant health consequences. Being uninsured or underinsured correlates to poorer quality of health care, lower rates of preventive care, and a greater probability of death. Uninsured adults are 25 percent more likely to die prematurely than adults with health insurance.[3]

Many people who are uninsured or underinsured avoid seeking medical care unless they are faced with an emergency, or they delay care until their symptoms become intolerable. As a result, the uninsured are less likely to receive a diagnosis in the early stages of a disease and are more likely to suffer complications from aggravated medical conditions.

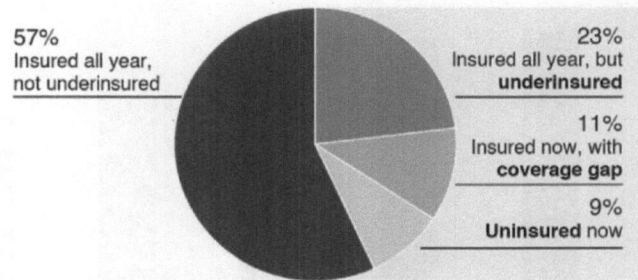

57%
Insured all year,
not underinsured

23%
Insured all year, but
underinsured

11%
Insured now, with
coverage gap

9%
Uninsured now

Figure 6.2   More Than Two of Five Working-Age Adults Are Inadequately Insured.

Source: Sara R. Collins, Lauren A. Haynes, and Relebohile Masitha, The State of U.S. Health Insurance in 2022: Findings from the Commonwealth Fund Biennial Health Insurance Survey *(Commonwealth Fund, Sept. 2022). https:// do.iorg/10.26099/73zg-3432*

They are at particular risk from diseases that are asymptomatic or produce only minor symptoms. People who don't have insurance are more likely to receive an initial diagnosis of cancer in the late stage of the disease and tend to have poorer treatment outcomes and to die within less time after diagnosis.

The lack of universal access to basic health services disproportionately affects marginalized communities. People of color and other disadvantaged groups experience avoidable disparities due to unequal access to health care. The lack of a right to health care perpetuates these inequities.[4]

The Cost of Not Being Covered

Here's a little-known fact. The number one reason Americans file for bankruptcy is not because they gamble or overspend on lavish lifestyles.

It's because they get sick.[5]

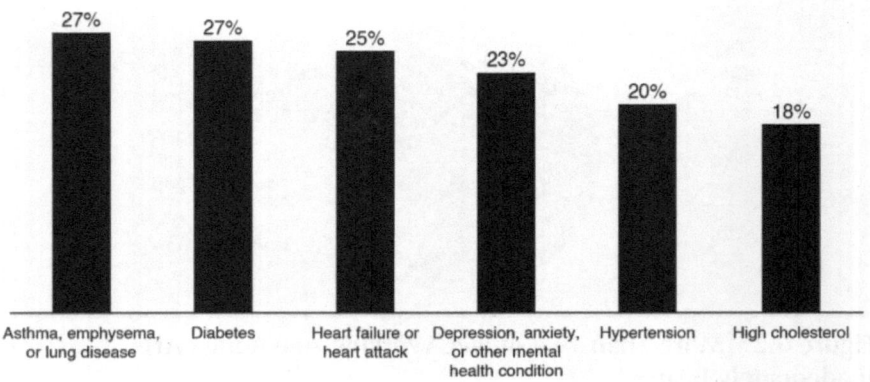

Figure 6.3   Percentage of Adults Ages 19–64 With a Chronic Condition Who Skipped or Didn't Fill a Prescription in the Past Year Because of Cost.

Source: Sara R. Collins, Lauren A. Haynes, and Relebohile Masitha, The State of U.S. Health Insurance in 2022: Findings from the Commonwealth Fund Biennial Health Insurance Survey *(Commonwealth Fund, Sept. 2022). https:// do.iorg/10.26099/73zg-3432*

Thousands of Americans are plunged into bankruptcy each year due to exorbitant medical expenses. One in seven working-age Americans has fallen behind on paying their medical bills. Beyond damaging credit ratings, medical debt discourages people from seeking the health care they need and interferes with their ability to afford basic necessities like food.[6]

Without universal access to health care, others face financial strain due to the high costs of treatments, medications, and hospital stays. The fear of medical bills looms large, deterring many from seeking necessary care and perpetuating a cycle of economic hardship.

And it's not just the uneducated and downtrodden who are impacted. It's all of us.

Leon Lederman was a University of Chicago professor who won a Nobel Prize for his pioneering physics research. He was the first to discover the subatomic particle, known as the "God particle." Later in life when he became ill, he was forced to sell his Nobel Prize medal for $765,000 to pay his mounting medical bills and stave off bankruptcy.[7]

When those who are un-or-underinsured eventually enter the system for care, the cost of providing this is eventually passed on to you, your employer, and other taxpayers in the form of higher prices for health care, goods and services, and taxes.

Which brings us to our next issue.

For Your Consideration:

1. Do you believe health care is a right or a privilege? If you believe it is a right, then what does this right include access to? All health and medical services available today or a basic set of services?
2. How important do you believe healthy citizens are to your community or society?
3. Have you or someone you know experienced challenges in accessing health care due to being uninsured or under-insured? How did this experience shape your perspective?

Notes:

_____

_____

_____

_____

_____

_____

_____

_____

_____

_____

_____

_____

_____

_____

_____

_____

_____

_____

_____

_____

Endnotes

1. Bianca Nwagbo, Colonial Medicine in the 18th Century, Smithsonian Learning Lab, https://learninglab.si.edu/collections/colonial-medicine-in-the-18th-century/A4UPfrbUuqaBohmy
2. State of U.S. Health Insurance in 2022: Biennial Survey, Commonwealth Fund, September 29, 2022, https://www.commonwealthfund.org/publications/issue-briefs/2022/sep/state-us-health-insurance-2022-biennial-survey
3. National Immigration Law Center, ISSUE BRIEF The Consequences of Being Uninsured, August, 2014, https://www.nilc.org/wp-content/uploads/2015/11/consequences-of-being-uninsured-2014-08.pdf
4. Robert H. Shmerling, MD, Is Our Health Care System Broken?, Harvard Health Publishing, July 13, 2021, https://www.health.harvard.edu/blog/is-our-healthcare-system-broken-202107132542
5. Lina Velikova, MD, PhD, The Truths & Myths Behind Medical Bankruptcies. *MedAlert Help*, January 14, 2022, https://medalerthelp.org/blog/medical-bankruptcies/
6. Early Experiences Implementing Medical Debt Protection Laws in Colorado, Illinois, Maryland, and New Mexico, The Commonwealth Fund Blog, October 30, 2024, https://www.commonwealthfund.org/blog/2024/early-experiences-implementing-medical-debt-protection-laws-colorado-illinois-maryland?utm_campaign=Controlling%20Health%20Care%20Costs&utm_medium=email&_hsenc=p2ANqtz-85v3bWb1Iiygaa668f70-s52MoGfN4CGSbNZ4yP20nxy5prx6bTlW7VyO3Qv5uxIQ9avdF9uTmYw7rv3Wr7nI7FPwZQa3LEl_Hu9ATLxORZbW75I0&_hsmi=331612780&utm_source=alert
7. Sarah Kliff, Nobel Prize-Winning Physicist Leon Loederman Sold His Medal for $765,000 to Pay Medical Bills, *Vox*, October 4, 2018, https://www.vox.com/health-care/2018/10/4/17936626/leon-lederman-nobel-prize-medical-bills

Chapter 7

Economic Whack-a-Mole—The Impact of Cost-Shifting

When health care is not deemed a right, or provisions for universal access are not in place, it gives rise to a process known as cost-shifting. It's health care's economic version of whack-a-mole that impacts all of us.

Those who are uninsured or underinsured still get sick. When they do, they often avoid or delay seeking help. As they put off treatments their health declines which makes the eventual cost of treatment higher.

Here's how it works:

1. **Uninsured Patients**: When uninsured patients receive medical care, they often cannot pay the full cost of services. Hospitals and doctors still need to cover their expenses for providing care to those who cannot pay, so they shift these costs elsewhere.

2. **Charging Insured Patients More**: To compensate for the unpaid bills from un-and-underinsured patients,

DOI: 10.4324/9781003600695-8

hospitals and doctors increase the prices they charge to those patients who are insured or self-pay. This means that if you have insurance, or paying for the care you receive, you are indirectly covering the costs of those without coverage.

3. **Higher Premiums**: This cost-shifting affects individual patients and the broader health care system. Insurers absorb these costs which have been "shifted" to them. They, in turn, pass on these higher costs to their policy-holders. As a result, premiums for health insurance plans rise, affecting what employers and individuals pay for coverage.

The result is that people with health insurance end up covering the costs for hospitals and doctors who lose money treating un-or-under insured patients or when government programs like Medicare and Medicaid don't pay enough.

Cost-shifting creates a complex web where the financial burden of caring is indirectly borne by those with insurance, leading to higher costs for everyone in the system. It also degrades the health and well-being of those who are un-or-underinsured.

Since 2000, hospitals have provided $745 billion in uncompensated care to their patients.[1] This is part of the hidden expense of cost-shifting that you are paying for whether or not you use the health system.

The Government Is in on the Game

Those with private health insurance not only pay for financial losses incurred when hospitals provide services to those without insurance, they also subsidize financial shortfalls from government payers such as Medicare (federal program for seniors) and Medicaid (program for people with limited resources). Here is how the government has gotten in on the cost-shifting game:

- In 2022 Medicare paid just 82 cents for every dollar spent by hospitals caring for Medicare patients that year. This resulted in $99.2 billion in Medicare underpayments that year alone.[2]
- Since it's the federal government the rates paid are non-negotiable.
- The financial shortfalls resulting from the federal government "shorting" hospitals adequate payments is then packaged, hidden and passed on to private payers like insurance companies and patients that pay their own bills.
- Financial shortfalls experienced by hospitals and doctors are significant. According to the Medicare Payment Advisory Committee (an independent congressional agency), hospitals experienced a negative 8.5% margin. This represents an underpayment to providers of $100 billion in 2020. Negative margins are expected to run even deeper going forward.[3]

To put these numbers into perspective, 94% of hospitals have half or more of their hospital (inpatient) days paid for by Medicare and Medicaid.

And so, when public payers such as Medicare and Medicaid reduce their payments to hospitals or when hospitals face an increased number of uninsured patients, they respond by raising the prices charged to private insurers and those who pay for health services (Figure 7.1).

Cost-shifting is a complex phenomenon with far-reaching consequences. It's a big part of why Americans pay more for health care but get less when it comes to outcomes and overall results.

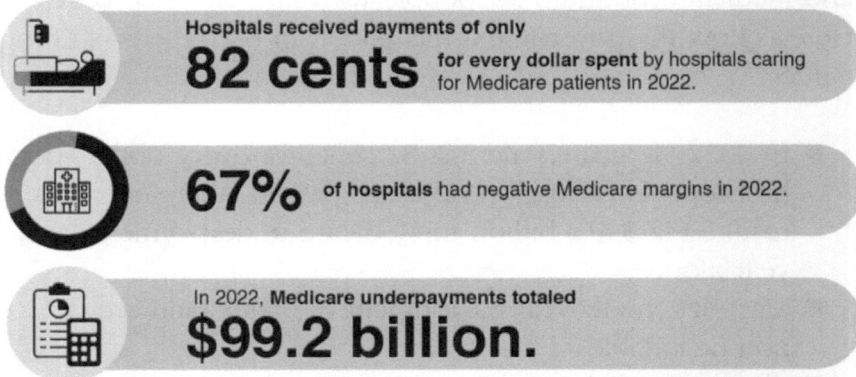

Figure 7.1   **Cost-shifting by Federal Government Impacts Prices Paid by Consumers and Employers.**

Source: American Hospital Association.

Cost-shifting also hides the costs of not having universal access and directly impacts financial sustainability, equitable access, and the quality of care and services everyone receives.[4]

When it comes to our investments in the system not producing a healthier population one only needs to understand the next issue to understand why.

For Your Consideration:

1. How does the concept of cost-shifting affect your view of the way health care operates in America? Does it make sense, or does it feel like a financial shell game?
2. How do you feel about the idea that people with insurance are indirectly paying for those who are uninsured or underinsured?
3. What changes, if any, do you think should be made to reduce the need for cost-shifting in the health care system?

Notes:

_____

_____

_____

_____

_____

_____

_____

_____

_____

_____

_____

_____

_____

_____

_____

_____

_____

Endnotes

1. Fact Sheet: Uncompensated Hospital Care Cost. *AHA*, February, 2022, https://www.vox.com/health-care/2018/10/4/17936626/leon-lederman-nobel-prize-medical-bills
   How Preventive Health care Services Reduce Spending for Payers (healthpayerintelligence.com)
2. Infographic: Medicare Significantly Underpays Hospitals for Cost of Patient Care. *AHA*, https://www.aha.org/2024-01-10-infographic-medicare-significantly-underpays-hospitals-cost-patient-care
3. Fact Sheet: Majority of Hospital Payments Dependent on Medicare or Medicaid. *AHA*, May 6, 2024, https://www.aha.org/fact-sheets/2022-05-25-fact-sheet-majority-hospital-payments-dependent-medicare-or-medicaid#:~:text=The%20Medicare%20Payment%20Advisory%20Commission%20found%20that%20hospitals,in%202020%2C%20up%20from%20%2476%20billion%20in%202019.
4. Shameek Rakshit, Krutika Amin, and Cynthia Cox, How Does Cost Affect Access to Health Care? – Peterson, KFF Health System Tracker, January 12, 2024, https://www.health-systemtracker.org/chart-collection/cost-affect-access-care/

Chapter 8

The Pervasive and Perversive Nature of a Break-Fix Model

Here are some things to consider:

> **Would you buy a new car from a company that only provided service once your vehicle stopped running?**
>
> **How about a computer company selling laptops that would only service your device once it was infected with a virus and rendered inoperable?**

As crazy as these examples sound, the American health care system essentially operates the same way. Today, 97% of our investments in health and medicine go to fixing things. Less than 3% goes to preventing bad things from happening in the first place.[1]

 DOI: 10.4324/9781003600695-9

While a few models in the United States financially incentivize keeping people healthy, the overwhelming majority of health and medical services are provided and paid for under what is known as a break-fix model (also known as fee-for-service).

This break-fix model is a *reactive approach* to health care. It's a system where:

- **Treatment occurs after a problem arises**: Patients seek medical attention when they are already sick or experiencing symptoms.
- **The focus is on fixing and healing rather than prevention and wellness**: Health care providers primarily address acute illnesses or injuries rather than emphasizing preventive measures.
- **A "Fee-for-service" payment structure drives costs**: Historically, health care reimbursement has been based on the number of services provided (such as doctor visits, tests, or procedures), rather than the outcomes achieved.
- **Transactional nature**: The system treats each medical encounter as a separate transaction rather than considering the patient's overall health journey.

There are many challenges in a break-fix model including:

1. **High costs**: Reactive care often leads to higher costs due to emergency room visits, hospitalizations, and late-stage interventions.
2. **Missed prevention opportunities**: By focusing less on prevention, the system misses opportunities to identify and address health risks early. For example, chronic diseases, many of which are avoidable through preventive

care services, account for 75% of the nation's health care spending in the US.[2]

3. **Fragmented care**: The transactional approach can result in fragmented care, where different providers handle different aspects of a patient's health without coordination.

4. **Inequities**: The model disproportionately affects vulnerable populations, as preventive and reactive care are often inaccessible or unaffordable.

The break-fix model incents the system to pay for *the volume of things done* rather than *the value we want from the system*. It accounts for every pill, lab test, and operation, whether or not any of that makes us healthier.

Economists and psychologists tell us that when people and systems are compensated for doing something independent of the results, they tend to do more of it.

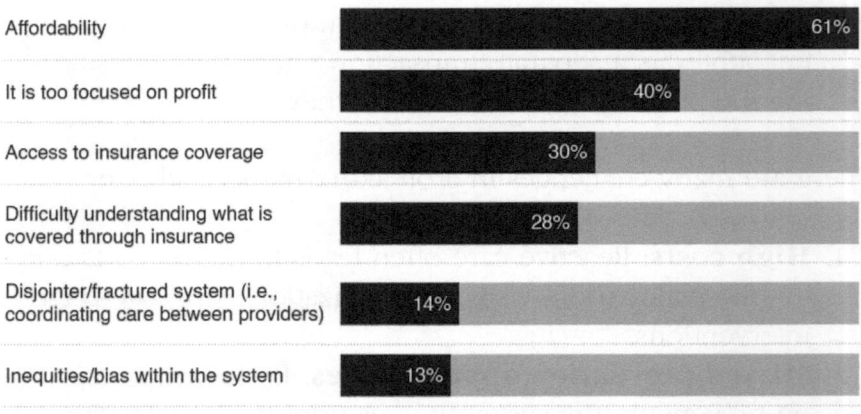

(2,519 people surveyed; survey-takers could select multiple options)

Affordability	61%
It is too focused on profit	40%
Access to insurance coverage	30%
Difficulty understanding what is covered through insurance	28%
Disjointer/fractured system (i.e., coordinating care between providers)	14%
Inequities/bias within the system	13%

Figure 8.1   What Do You Consider to be the Biggest Barriers to Access to Health Care in the U.S. Healthcare System?

Source: TIME-Harris Poll, https://time.com/6279937/us-health-care-system-attitudes/

Two Important Numbers to Understand Are 5 and 50

Health care expenditures are often cited as the amount of money spent per citizen or per capita. In America the latest number is that, on average, we spend $14,570 per citizen.[3]

It's important to recognize that this is an *average.* This number often shades the real truth of where the money *actually* goes. Or as Mark Twain quipped—*There are three kinds of lies: Lies, damned lies, and statistics.*

To better understand where most of the money goes, take your eyes off of the per capita spending numbers that are bantered about and consider this:

> ***50 percent of American health expenditures go towards treating just 5 percent of Americans.***[4]

Additionally, it's worth noting that 24% of all health care spending in America is directed toward a mere 1% of the population.[5]

What this means is that health care spending is highly concentrated on a very small number of high-cost users.[6]

At the other end of the spending spectrum, half of America's population accounts for just 3% of total health care spending (Figure 8.2).

The data suggests that each year, the health problems of about 15 million Americans consume almost one-tenth of the US' Gross Domestic Product (GDP).[7]

In other countries, resources are also spent on a small number of very sick citizens, but the US stands out for focusing a disproportionately large number of resources on a few patients compared to any other nation.

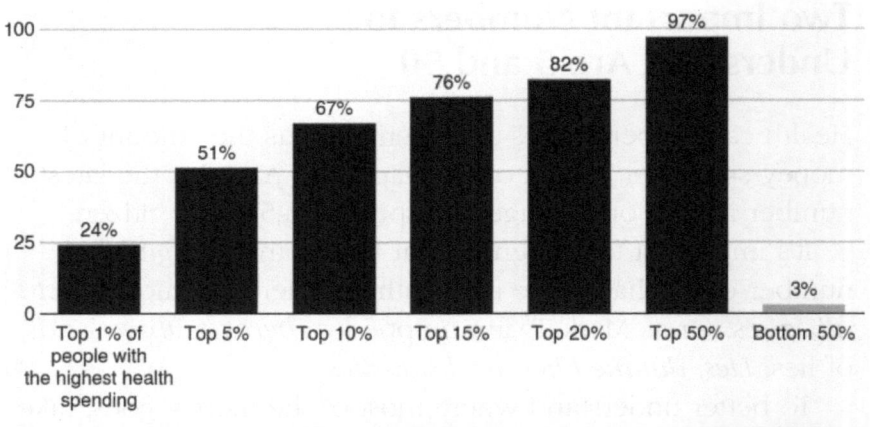

Figure 8.2   Share of Total Health Spending, by Percentile, 2021.

Source: KFF analysis of 2021 Medical Expenditure Panel Survey data. Get the data PNG.

Understanding the impact of universal access, cost-shifting, and the break-fix model is foundational to creating a more proactive, preventive approach to a sustainable and effective health care system in America.

These major trends are complex and have wide-ranging effects. Balancing financial sustainability, fair access, and high-quality care is a major challenge for the U.S. health care system.

To address the issues of universal access, cost-shifting, and misguided financial incentives, we need thoughtful policies and a collaborative approach to new models that achieve better health outcomes for all Americans.[8]

For Your Consideration:

1. What are the long-term consequences of a health care system that prioritizes treating illnesses over preventing them?
2. Would your own health care behaviors change if the system prioritized prevention and wellness over treatments after illness?
3. How does the concentration of health care spending on a small percentage of the population reflect on our societal values and priorities? Would you change this?
4. Should the government and the private sector play a role in shifting from a break-fix model to a preventive model in health care? What would this look like? What might it include?

Notes:

_____

_____

_____

_____

_____

_____

_____

_____

_____

_____

_____

_____

_____

_____

_____

Endnotes

1. Rabah Kamal and Julie Hudman, What Do We Know About Spending Related to Public Health in the U.S. and Comparable Countries? September 30, 2020, Peterson-KFF Health System Tracker, https://www.healthsystemtracker.org/chart-collection/what-do-we-know-about-spending-related-to-public-health-in-the-u-s-and-comparable-countries/#Preventive%20care%20spending%20by%20government/compulsory%20schemes%20as%20a%20share%20of%20total%20national%20health%20expenditures,%202000-2018

2. Emma Wager, Matthew McGough, Shameek Rakshit, Krutika Amin, and Cynthia Cox, How Does Health Spending in the U.S. Compare to Other Countries? Peterson-KFF Health System Tracker. January 23, 2024. https://www.healthsystemtracker.org/chart-collection/health-spending-u-s-compare-countries/

3. "Understanding U.S. Health Care Spending". National Institute of Health care Management, July, 2011. http://www.bcnys.org/inside/health/2011/Health carePremiumsNIHCM0711.pdf

4. Emily M. Mitchell, PhD, Concentration of Health Expenditures in the U.S. Civilian Noninstitutionalized Population, 2014, Agency for Healthcare Research and Quality's (AHRQ) Medical Expenditure Panel Survey, November 2016, https://meps.ahrq.gov/data_files/publications/st497/stat497.pdf

5. "The High Concentration of U.S. Health Care Expenditures". Agency for Health care Research and Quality, https://archive.ahrq.gov/research/findings/factsheets/costs/expriach/

6. Statistical Brief #533: Concentration of Healthcare Expenditures and Selected Characteristics of Persons with High Expenses, U.S. Civilian Noninstitutionalized Population, 2018. Agency for Healthcare Research and Quality (AHRQ), January 2021, https://meps.ahrq.gov/data_files/publications/st533/stat533.shtml

7. Emma Wager, Matthew McGough, Shameek Rakshit, Krutika Amin, and Cynthia Cox, How Does Health Spending in the U.S. Compared to Other Countries? Peterson-KFF Health System Tracker. January 23, 2024, 37.

Chapter 9

The Price of Self-Inflicted Disease

"The greatest gift you can give your family and the world is a healthy you."

—Joyce Meyer

An issue as big as health care is the environment. And so, what if there was a way to dramatically improve the health of all Americans while decreasing our consumption of fossil fuels by a billion gallons a year?

Transformational new technology? Innovative legislation from Washington? Actually, the answer is simple. We would achieve these goals by reducing the weight of the average American to what it was in 1962.[1]

Sheldon Jacobson is a computer science professor who has studied the effects of obesity and fuel consumption. His work points to a simple matter of physics. Heavier drivers increase fuel consumption. Car engines burn more energy to move more weight. The added weight Americans have packed on since the sixties costs motorists an estimated $4 billion a year.[2]

DOI: 10.4324/9781003600695-10

The Rise of Diet-Related Chronic Diseases

Diet-related chronic diseases have reached an alarming prevalence among Americans. As a result, the majority of U.S. adults are not healthy.

More than 37 million Americans have diabetes, and another 96 million adults have a condition called pre-diabetes. One hundred and twenty-two million suffer from high blood pressure, and 42% suffer from obesity.[3,4]

The cost of treating diet-related diseases is enormous. Heart disease, type 2 diabetes, and obesity together are estimated to cost Americans over $700 billion per year just in health care costs.[5,6]

Lost productivity costs for diet-related diseases meanwhile exceed $1 trillion per year. Beyond productivity, these numbers do not measure the impact on individuals and families due to lost quality of life.

In the rest of this chapter, we'll use obesity to illustrate how diet-related chronic diseases impact both our health and our wallet.

Supersizing America

Americans are being "supersized" at an alarming rate as part of a global obesity pandemic that is driven by a variety of lifestyle and environmental factors. Around the world, more people now die from obesity than malnutrition. It has overtaken tobacco as the largest cause of preventable disease.[7]

Obesity is a *real* disease recognized by the American Medical Association, World Health Organization and others. Like smoking, and overreliance on alcohol and drugs, it is a non-communicable disease.

Communicable diseases, like flu, COVID, and measles are caused by forces in nature.

Non-communicable diseases are influenced by many factors beyond our personal control like genetics or exposure to hazardous materials in the environment. They are also influenced, in some manner, by choices we make as consumers. These choices, in turn, are heavily influenced by external societal forces.[8]

Obesity currently affects 4 out of 10 Americans, according to data from the Centers for Disease Control and Prevention (CDC).[9] By 2030, if nothing changes, one in two American adults will have obesity and one in four will have severe obesity.[10]

Socioeconomic factors, such as income, education, and access to health care, play a significant role in determining obesity rates. For example, obesity is more pervasive among low-income Americans and minorities.[11] It is less prevalent among men and women with college degrees compared with those with less education.[12] (More on the importance of Social Determinants of Health in the next chapter).

Beyond its direct impact, obesity is a gateway disease. It's been the main driver of diabetes in America for the last two decades. It contributes to about half of new diabetes cases annually in the United States.[13]

Obesity also increases the prevalence of cardiovascular disease, cancer, osteoarthritis, infertility, sleep apnea, and other health conditions.[14]

A Heavy Price Paid by All

Obesity is not only bad for our health but also very expensive.

Worldwide, obesity has the same economic impact as smoking or armed conflict.[15]

Within the US, the annual medical cost of obesity is $173 billion annually. Medical costs for adults who have obesity are $1,861 higher on average than medical costs for people with healthy weight.[16]

On average Americans who are obese, spend more on medical services and medications than smokers and heavy drinkers.[17] They incur 40% higher inpatient hospital costs, 27% more physician visits and outpatient costs and consume 80% more prescription drugs.[18]

Beyond direct medical costs, obesity impacts the productivity and competitiveness of America's employers and workforce. Businesses incur higher costs for disability and unemployment benefits and face additional costs associated with obesity-related job absenteeism and lost productivity.

For example, a study by the Society of Actuaries estimates that U.S. employers are losing $164 billion in productivity each year due to obesity-related issues with employees.[19] The Robert Wood Johnson Foundation predicts that annual economic productivity loss due to obesity is likely to reach $550 billion by 2030.[20]

Without significant change, obesity-related costs will rise dramatically, with increases being absorbed by consumers, employers, and the goods and services they provide.

Consumers will be increasingly impacted by larger out-of-pocket expenses as well as higher taxes to support programs such as Medicare and Medicaid. Because of their national price tag, these programs are already teetering on the brink of disaster. One study notes that 21% of Medicare recipients had a diagnosis of diabetes in 2019 compared to just 6.2% in 2010.[21]

Solving for Obesity Is Simple and Complex

When it comes to understanding what is driving obesity in the US, and what can be done to slow or stop this epidemic, the answer is both simple and complex.

At a simple level, the obesity epidemic is caused by Americans consuming more calories through food and

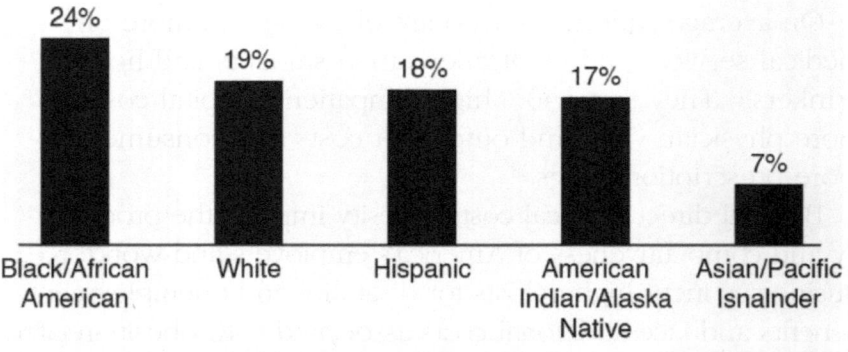

Figure 9.1 Prevalence of Obesity Among Medicare Beneficiaries by Race/Ethnicity.

Source: Centers for Disease Control and Prevention. Adult Obesity Facts. https://www.cdc.gov/obesity/data/adult.html

beverages than they expend. But as anyone who has ever tried to go on a diet knows, it's much more than that.

The deeper answer to why this is occurring is rooted in a myriad of issues that have unfolded over the past few decades.

Today, we live in a world where inactive lifestyles are the norm and inexpensive, high calorie foods and drinks are readily available 24 hours a day.

There are fewer safe places to walk or play. Some of our communities (especially low-income neighborhoods) lack affordable, healthy food outlets. Advertisements for unhealthy foods and beverages constantly bombard us.

Let's look at how these societal trends are impacting our children, who without some types of intervention are already on their way to being the obese patients we will care and pay for in the decades to come.

Today about 20% of U.S. children have obesity—almost 15 million children whose lives will be shorter and of lower quality. The prevalence of obesity in children has more than tripled since 1971 and is now the number one health concern among parents in the US, topping drug abuse and smoking.[22]

Even the youngest children are not spared. About 20% of children are already overweight or obese before they enter school, and rates are even higher among low-income, African American and Latino children.[23]

If you are a parent, there are many reasons to be concerned. Obesity is causing a broad range of new health problems in children that previously weren't seen until adulthood. These include high blood pressure, type 2 diabetes and elevated blood cholesterol levels. Fatty liver disease now afflicts 5-10% of all U.S. children, about the same number of children who have asthma, one of the most common chronic conditions in childhood.[24,25]

There are also psychological effects: Obese children are more prone to low self-esteem, negative body image and depression.[26]

If you are a parent and want your child to be healthy, it would seem reasonable that there are several simple things to do to ensure that they are not overweight or obese. For example, a study from the American Journal of Preventive Medicine found that eliminating just 41 calories a day could halt rising body weight trends in children and teens.[27]

Unfortunately, environmental forces work against achieving what appears to be a simple goal.

Today children are less active than at any point in our history.

Every day kids aged 8–18, on average, spend a whopping 7.5 hours in front of a screen for entertainment. Over a year, that adds up to 114 full days watching a screen for fun. It doesn't include the time they spent on a computer at school for educational purposes or at home for homework.[28]

In 1969, half of all children walked or biked to school. Today, about 13% walk or bike to school.[29]

Want to know what movie will be the next box office hit among kids? Look at the promotional toys and ads being served up by fast-food companies. They specialize in marketing to kids and adolescents.

In one study by the Robert Wood Johnson Foundation, McDonald's was found to have the strongest emphasis on the children's market, with 40% of 44,062 ads studied aimed at kids.[30] Beyond the blitz of airtime focused on children, the fast-food companies use free toys and popular movies to appeal to kids by focusing on promotions, brands, and logos—not on food."[31]

As a result, on any given day, 34.3% of U.S. children eat pizza, fried chicken, tacos, or some other dish prepared in a fast-food restaurant.[32] French fries are now the most common *"vegetable"* that kids eat, making up 25% of American children's total vegetable intake.[33]

And so, whether you are an adult trying to lose weight, or a parent wanting a healthy future for your children, there are many environmental and societal forces that are working against you.

Highlighting the consequences of obesity in America illustrates the opportunity to create a health system that supports prevention rather than dealing with the downstream effects and costs that currently fill hospital beds, cost billions of dollars and robs many citizens of their health.

Another study by the Robert Wood Johnson Foundation notes that if we could lower obesity trends by reducing the average adult BMI (body mass index) by only 5 percent in each state, we could spare millions of Americans from serious health problems and save billions of dollars in health spending.[34,35]

Let's go back to the story about cars and overweight drivers. A recent study examined the health benefits of taking public transit instead of driving. It showed that taking public transit is associated with walking 8.3 more minutes per day on average. This burns an additional 26–39 calories per day (as a comparison, burning an additional 100 calories per day would help 90% of Americans from becoming obese).[36]

The additional walking associated with public transit could save $5,500 per person in present value by reducing obesity-related medical costs. Savings in quality-adjusted life years could be even higher.[37]

Creating a system that addresses obesity in Americans offers a wide range of benefits, including lowering the risk of chronic diseases, alleviating the burden on health care systems, improving mental health and well-being, boosting economic productivity, and promoting equity and social justice.

Obesity serves as an example of what might be done for other diet-related chronic conditions. By prioritizing prevention efforts at the individual, community, and policy levels, we can create a healthier, happier, and more prosperous society for all.

For Your Consideration:

1. Should the government play a stronger role in preventing or mitigating self-inflicted health issues that impact health and increase costs (Similar to what it did with smoking and seat belt laws)? If yes, how far should such actions go?
2. In the example of obesity, would changes like the greater availability of healthy foods and more safe spaces for physical activity reduce the prevalence of obesity? What actions would encourage healthier habits to prevent or reduce the prevalence of diet-related health issues?
3. Do you think public health campaigns or community-based interventions are effective in promoting and achieving healthier lifestyles? Why or why not?
4. Should things like weight loss programs or vouchers for healthy foods be included in health benefits?

Notes:

_____

_____

_____

_____

_____

_____

_____

_____

_____

_____

_____

_____

_____

_____

Endnotes

1. Sheldon Jackson (2006, 2008), The Engineering Economist. "The Economic Impact of Obesity on Automobile Fuel Consumption," published in *The Engineering Economist,* 51(4), 307–323.
2. Sheldon Jackson (2006, 2008), The Engineering Economist. "The Economic Impact of Obesity on Automobile Fuel Consumption," published in *The Engineering Economist,* 51(4), 307–323.
3. National Center for Chronic Disease Prevention and Health Promotion. (2022 December 13). Chronic Diseases in America. Centers for Disease Control and Prevention.
4. National Center for Chronic Disease Prevention and Health Promotion. (2023 March 23). Health and Economic Costs of Chronic Diseases. Centers for Disease Control and Prevention.
5. National Center for Chronic Disease Prevention and Health Promotion. (2024 July 12). Fast Facts: Health and Economic Costs of Chronic Conditions. Centers for Disease Control and Prevention.
6. National Center for Chronic Disease Prevention and Health Promotion. (2024 May 15). Health and Economic Benefits of Diabetes Interventions. Centers for Disease Control and Prevention.
7. Chong, Bryan et al., Trends and Predictions of Malnutrition and Obesity in 204 Countries and Territories: An Analysis of the Global Burden of Disease Study 2019. *eClinicalMedicine*, 57, 101850.
8. Non Communicable Diseases Fact Sheet, (2013), World Health Organization, http://www.who.int/mediacentre/factsheets/fs355/en/
9. Adult Obesity Facts, CDC, May 14, 2024, https://www.cdc.gov/obesity/php/data-research/adult-obesity-facts.html?CDC_AAref_Val=https://www.cdc.gov/obesity/data/adult.html
10. Chloe Duvall, MD, Kunal Jha, MD, Roger S. Blumenthal, MD, FACC, Roberta Florido, MD, The Myriad Cardiovascular Effects of Obesity, American College of Cardiology, July 16, 2021, https://www.acc.org/latest-in-cardiology/articles/2021/07/15/19/32/the-myriad-cardiovascular-effects-of-obesity
11. Trust for America's Health and Robert Wood Johnson Foundation. F as in Fat: How Obesity Threatens America's Future — 2011, http://www.tfah.org/report/88/ (accessed July 2012). Based on data using the previous BRFSS methodology in use from 2008 to 2010.

12. Adult Obesity Facts, CDC, 54.
13. Obesity Contributes to Up to Half of New Diabetes Cases Annually in the United States, American Heart Association, February 10, 2021, https://newsroom.heart.org/news/obesity-contributes-to-up-to-half-of-new-diabetes-cases-annually-in-the-united-states
14. Y Claire Wang, Klim McPerhson, Tim Marsh, Steven L. Gortmaker, and Martin Brown. Health and Economic Burden of the Projected Obesity Trends in the USA and the UK. *The Lancet*, 2011, 815–827.
15. Overcoming Obesity: An Initial Economic Analysis, McKinsey Global Institute, November 2014, http://www.mckinsey.com/Insights/Economic_Studies/How_the_world_could_better_fight_obesity
16. Adult Obesity Facts, CDC, 54.
17. Roland Sturm. The Effects of Obesity, Smoking, and Problem Drinking on Chronic Medical Problems and Health Care Costs. *Health Affairs*, 21(2), 2002, 245–253.
18. Roland Sturm. The Effects of Obesity, Smoking, and Problem Drinking on Chronic Medical Problems and Health Care Costs. *Health Affairs,* 21(2), 2002, 245–253.
19. Overweight and Obesity Study. Society of Actuaries, 2009, https://www.soa.org/Research/Research-At-A-Glance.aspx
20. Trust for America's Health and Robert Wood Johnson Foundation. F as in Fat: How Obesity Threatens America's Future — 2011.
21. Medicare Tables & Reports—Chronic Conditions Data Warehouse, CMS, https://www2.ccwdata.org/web/guest/medicare-tables-reports
22. Overweight in Children, American Heart Association, www.heart.org/HEARTORG/HealthyLiving/HealthyKids/ChildhoodObesity/Overweight-in-Children_UCM_304054_Article.jsp#.WGavuWwzWbg
23. Early Childhood Obesity Prevention Policies. Institute of Medicine, https://www.nap.edu/download/13124
24. E.L. Yu, and J.B. Schwimmer. Epidemiology of Pediatric Nonalcoholic Fatty Liver Disease. *PubMed Central*, 7(3), 2021, April 13, 196–199.
25. E.L. Yu, and J.B. Schwimmer. Epidemiology of Pediatric Nonalcoholic Fatty Liver Disease. *PubMed Central*, 7(3), 2021, April 13, 196–199.

26. Overweight in Children, American Heart Association, www.heart.org/HEARTORG/HealthyLiving/HealthyKids/ChildhoodObesity/Overweight-in-Children_UCM_304054_Article.jsp#.WGavuWwzWbg

27. Y. Claire Wang, C. Tracy Orleans, and Steven L. Gortmaker. Reaching the Healthy People Goals for Reducing Childhood Obesity: Closing the Energy Gap. *American Journal of Preventive Medicine*, https://doi.org/10.1016/j.amepre.2012.01.018, 2012.

28. Generation M2 – Media in the Lives of 8 to 18 Year Olds, Kaiser Family Foundation, January 2010, https://www2.ccw-data.org/web/guest/medicare-tables-reports

29. The National Center for Safe Routes to School, 2011, http://guide.saferoutesinfo.org/introduction/the_decline_of_walking_and_bicycling.cfm

30. Fast-Food Television Ads Use Toys, Movies to Target Kids. Robert Wood Johnson Foundation, April 2013, http://www.rwjf.org/en/library/articles-and-news/2013/08/fast-food-television-ads-use-toys--movies-to-target-kids.html

31. Fast-Food Television Ads Use Toys, Movies to Target Kids. Robert Wood Johnson Foundation, April 2013, http://www.rwjf.org/en/library/articles-and-news/2013/08/fast-food-television-ads-use-toys--movies-to-target-kids.html

32. Caloric Intake from Fast Food Among Children and Adolescents in the United States, 2011–2012. Centers for Disease Control, September 2015, https://www.cdc.gov/nchs/data/databriefs/db213.htm

33. Obesity in Infants to Preschoolers. American Heart Association. http://www.heart.org/HEARTORG/HealthyLiving/HealthyKids/ChildhoodObesity/Obesity-in-Infants-and-Preschoolers-Infographic_UCM_467593_SubHomePage.jsp

34. Body Measurements, National Center for Health Statistics. https://www.cdc.gov/nchs/fastats/body-measurements.htm

35. F as in Fat: How Obesity Threatens America's Future. Trust for America's Health (TFAH) and the Robert Wood Johnson Foundation. 2012.

36. Ryan D Edwards, Public Transit, Obesity, and Medical Costs: Assessing the Magnitudes, National Library of Medicine, January, 2008, https://pubmed.ncbi.nlm.nih.gov/18037480/

37. Ryan D Edwards, Public Transit, Obesity, and Medical Costs: Assessing the Magnitudes, National Library of Medicine, January, 2008, https://pubmed.ncbi.nlm.nih.gov/18037480/

Chapter 10

Health Is More than Medicine

"Where you live should not determine whether you live."

—*Bono*

When it comes to things that impact your health status here's a question: Which is a better predictor of health—your genetic code or your zip code?

While both are important, where you live affects how you live. It impacts whether you have access to healthy food, places to exercise, clean air and water, or health services when needed.

Your *"living location"* also affects your personal and family's economic prosperity based on the availability of jobs, unemployment rates, and educational and training opportunities. These *"social"* factors impact health and longevity across your lifespan.

In our quest to envision and pursue a new model for health and well-being, a profound shift must occur to look beyond traditional medical interventions and encompass a broader

DOI: 10.4324/9781003600695-11

perspective known as the Social Determinants of Health (SDOH).

This approach recognizes that social, economic and environmental factors significantly influence health outcomes. It highlights the interconnectedness of various aspects of individuals' lives with their overall well-being.

Change these factors and you change health status at scale.

The World Health Organization defines social determinants of health as *the conditions in which people are born, grow, work, live, and age, and the wider set of forces and systems shaping the conditions of daily life.*[1]

In many ways, social determinants of health are a commonsense approach to positively impacting health. It focuses on changing and improving the conditions in which people live.

For example, without access to grocery stores with healthy foods (known as food deserts), nutrition suffers, raising the risk of health conditions like heart disease, diabetes, and obesity. Such things contribute to lower life expectancy relative to people who have access to healthy foods.

Food deserts are areas where residents have limited access to affordable and nutritious food, often due to lack of grocery stores or other healthy food providers. Addressing this issue and improving access to healthy foods is a factor that could significantly influence the prevalence of obesity and other diet-related diseases, as we covered in the last chapter.

The idea for how to use SDOH is straightforward. If we work to reshape community and environmental factors that adversely impact health, we can help more people be healthy throughout their lives while decreasing our reliance and expenditures on a system designed to fix people after they are ill or injured.

As we learned in Chapter 8, the American health care system operates mainly as a break-fix model. This model typically does not factor in SDOH in managing a condition or illness.

Here's an example:

Two 60-year-old women live 10 miles apart in the
Washington, DC area. When examining the typical
information health systems gather and use to man-
age the care of patients, these women appear to be
identical. They've both been prescribed beta-blockers
for high blood pressure, both have family histories of
Type 2 diabetes, and both have missed their last few
annual check-ups.

Shouldn't the plan to manage their health be the same? One
additional piece of data dramatically tilts the equation. It's their
zip code. Based on their location, one will likely live 33 years
longer (63 years versus 96).[2] This dramatic life expectancy gap
can be chalked up to differences in things like income, education, and access to grocery stores with fresh food.

Social and environmental factors are much more indicative
of a person's health and health outcome than once thought.
One study suggests that 60% of a person's health care outcome is driven by their behavior and social and economic factors, 10% by their clinical care, and 30% by their genetics.[3]

The Color of Coronavirus

Neighborhoods with large populations of African Americans
tend to have lower life expectancies than majority White,
Hispanic, or Asian communities. Such racial differences reflect
the places where different races live, not the individual characteristics of people themselves.[4]

COVID helped give voice to this issue.

At the beginning of the pandemic, Black Americans were
twice more likely to die from COVID than White Americans
even though they were a smaller percentage of the overall
population. In taking a closer look at the situation, two things
became clear.

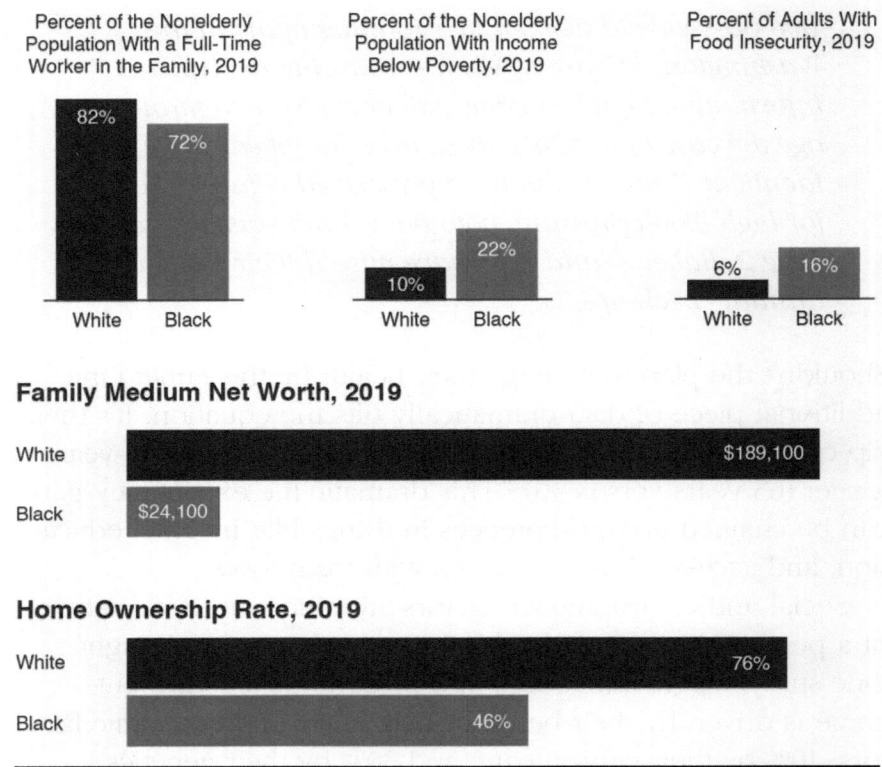

Figure 10.1   Black People Are More Likely than White People to Face Social and Economic Inequities That Negatively Impact Health.

Source: Kaiser Family Foundation.

First, higher death rates related to where people lived. Second, the *"twice as likely to die"* was a statistical average. Underneath this average was the true story. If you were Black and living in Washington, DC, you were six times more likely to die of COVID at that time. Living in Michigan meant that you were four times more likely to die of COVID.[5]

Black communities are less likely to have access to resources that promote health, like grocery stores with fresh foods, places to exercise, and quality health care facilities. This is true even in middle-class neighborhoods.[6,7,8]

These communities also have fewer opportunities for economic prosperity, with higher unemployment rates and fewer opportunities to work and lower quality education, all of which shape health outcomes across a lifespan.

The Economics for Health

How well a community does economically affects how long people can expect to live. Financially distressed areas tend to have the lowest life expectancies.[9] Research from the Census Bureau and researchers at Harvard and Brown Universities shows that children from financially disadvantaged neighborhoods tend to have worse outcomes as adults.[10]

These data demonstrate the importance of understanding and factoring SDOH into planning and delivering health services.

Health disparities are not merely the result of individual behavior; they stem from decades of systematic inequality in economic, housing, and health care systems.

Understanding the importance of social determinants of health is crucial for several reasons:

Health Inequalities: SDOH shed light on the disparities in health outcomes among different populations. Individuals from marginalized communities, including racial and ethnic minorities and low-income groups, often face more significant challenges in achieving and maintaining good health. Addressing social determinants is essential for tackling these health inequities and promoting health equity for all.

Holistic Health Approach: By considering social determinants, health and other social service organizations can collaborate and create a more comprehensive and holistic approach to helping citizens manage their health.

Rather than solely focusing on treating diseases, health care systems, government entities and the private sector can address the underlying factors contributing to health issues, such as poverty, inadequate housing, or food insecurity. This approach improves individual health outcomes and also enhances overall community well-being.

Preventive Health Care: Social determinants play a significant role in shaping health behaviors and outcomes. Preventive interventions can be implemented to promote healthier lifestyles and reduce the burden of chronic diseases by addressing factors such as food deserts.

Cost Savings: Investing in addressing social determinants of health can lead to substantial cost savings in the long run. By preventing health problems before they escalate and reducing the need for expensive medical treatments, interventions aimed at improving social and economic conditions can result in more efficient use of health care resources and lower health care costs for individuals, families, and society as a whole.

A Call to Action Starts with Public Policy

Recognizing the importance of social determinants of health has significant implications for public policy and decision-making. Efforts to address social determinants of health require collaboration across multiple sectors, including health care, social services, education, housing, and employment.

Community-based organizations, government agencies, health care providers, researchers, and policymakers all have a role to play in identifying and implementing effective interventions to mitigate the impact of social determinants on health.

Policies aimed at improving education, housing, employment opportunities, income equality, and access to health care can have far-reaching effects on population health outcomes.

Creating a cost-effective health system that benefits all citizens starts with understanding that addressing social determinants of health is essential for promoting health equity, improving health outcomes, and reducing health care costs.

Health doesn't solely depend on medical interventions; it builds from where we live, learn, work, and play.

For Your Consideration:

1. How do you think your living environment influences your health and well-being? What changes could you make to improve these factors?
2. Reflect on how socioeconomic factors, such as income and education, impact your life and those around you. How might these factors affect your health outcomes and those of your community?
3. In what ways could recognizing and addressing social determinants of health change the way we approach health care?
4. Reflect on the economic impacts of health disparities discussed in the chapter. How might improving social determinants of health lead to cost savings and better health outcomes? What steps might policymakers and communities take to achieve these goals?

Notes:

_____

_____

_____

_____

_____

_____

_____

_____

_____

_____

_____

_____

_____

Endnotes

1. Social Determinants of Health, World Health Organization, https://www.who.int/health-topics/social-determinants-of-health#tab=tab_1
2. Greg Kefer, Zip Codes Have Become a Better Predictor of Health Outcomes Than Genetic Codes. Technology May Be Ready to Fix That. *Medcity News*, August 24, 2021, https://medcitynews.com/2021/08/zip-codes-have-become-a-better-predictor-of-health-outcomes-than-genetic-codes-technology-may-be-ready-to-fix-that
3. S.A. Shroeder. We Can Do Better – Improving the Health of the American People. *NEJM*, 357, 2007, 1221–1228.
4. U.S. Small-Area Life Expectancy Estimates Project: Methodology and Results Summary, NATIONAL CENTER FOR HEALTH STATISTICS, September 2018. https://www.cdc.gov/nchs/data/series/sr_02/sr02_181.pdf
5. APM Research Lab. The Color of Coronavirus: COVID-19 Deaths by Race and Ethnicity in the U.S. Data Updated as of June 10, 2020, https://www.apmresearchlab.org/covid/deaths-by-race
6. APM Research Lab. The Color of Coronavirus: COVID-19 Deaths by Race and Ethnicity in the U.S. Data Updated as of June 10, 2020, https://www.apmresearchlab.org/covid/deaths-by-race
7. Nicole I. Larson, Mary T. Story, and Melissa C. Nelson. Neighborhood Environments Disparities in Access to Healthy Foods in the U.S. *American Journal of Preventive Medicine*, November 03, 2008, https://doi.org/10.1016/j.amepre.2008.09.025
8. Ray Rayshawn, An Intersectional Analysis to Explaining a Lack of Physical Activity Among Middle Class Black Women Wiley Online Library, September 2014, https://doi.org/10.1111/soc4.12172
9. When It Comes to Your Health, Where You Live Matters. The Conversation, January 2018. https://theconversation.com/when-it-comes-to-your-health-where-you-live-matters-89352
10. Detailed Maps Show How Neighborhoods Shape Children for Life. The New York Times, October 1, 2018, https://www.nytimes.com/2018/10/01/upshot/maps-neighborhoods-shape-child-poverty.html

Chapter 11

What Would
Martin Think?

"Of all the forms of inequality, injustice in health care
is the most shocking and inhuman."

—*Martin Luther King Jr.*

I was going to start this chapter with a story as I have in previous chapters, but instead, I thought it best to begin with this simple truth:

Being a person of color in America can be harmful to your health.

Despite strides made, we remain engaged in an important societal debate about entrenched inequalities and the impact such disparities have on Black Americans, Hispanics, and others. Nowhere is this more evident than in our approach to health.

Racial disparities in health care exist today. This is not a political point of view but an important humanitarian issue. It's the conclusion of the Institute of Medicine's (IOM) study, *Unequal Treatment: Confronting Racial and Ethnic*

Disparities in Health Care. This study, along with many others, documents measurable differences in the quality of health care received by racial and ethnic minorities and non-minorities.[1]

Health disparities refer to the unequal distribution of health outcomes across different racial and ethnic groups. They lead to significant differences in health status and outcomes and impact the generational transfer of *physical and economic* health and well-being.

These disparities are deeply rooted in historical, social, and economic factors that are collectively referred to as *structural racism.* This is where a system of policies, practices, and norms perpetuate racial inequality and disadvantage certain racial or ethnic groups.

Unlike individual acts of racism, which involve overt prejudice or discrimination by individuals, structural racism operates at a broader level. It's embedded within the institutions and systems of a society.

When it comes to health disparities, Black Americans are generally at higher risk for heart diseases, stroke, cancer, asthma, influenza and pneumonia, diabetes, and HIV/AIDS compared to their White counterparts.[2]

Even though Black Americans have a lower rate of cancer incidence compared to Whites, their death rate for all cancers is higher. This is due to a combination of factors.[3,4] Cancer screening rates are lower.[5] They receive later -stage diagnoses for many types of cancers. Racial disparities in cancer care and treatment have also been identified, particularly for diagnostic and treatment delays, which contribute to worse survival outcomes.[6]

Black children have a 500% higher death rate from asthma compared with White children. Meanwhile, Hispanic women are 2.5 times less likely to receive no prenatal care.[7,8]

Two-thirds of Black and Hispanic children, currently aged 2 to 19, are projected to be obese by the age of 35, compared to the national average of 57%.[9]

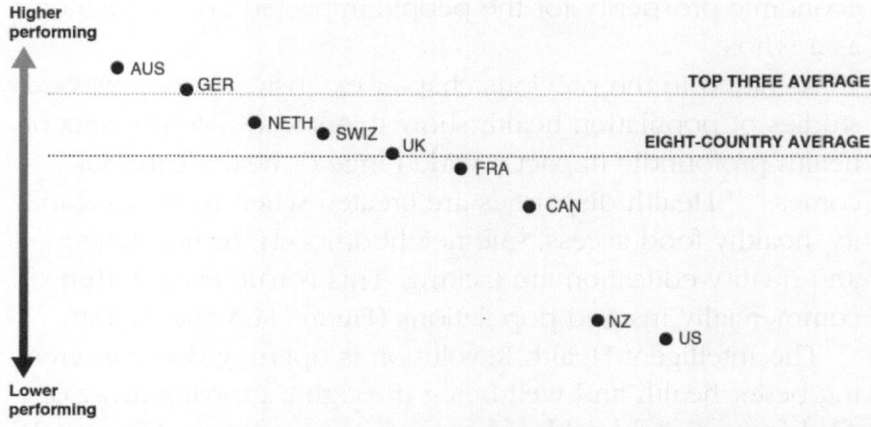

Figure 11.1   The U.S. Trails Its Peers for Equity in Health Care Access and Experience.

Source: David Blumenthal et al., Mirror, Mirror 2024: A Portrait of the Falling US Health System – Comparing Performance in 10 Nations *(Commonwealth Fund, Sept. 2024). hnps://doi.org/10.26099/ta0g-zp66*

The list goes on. A complete accounting of health dispari-ties would fill this book. Health disparities in America run deep. They harm people and create holes in the fabric of

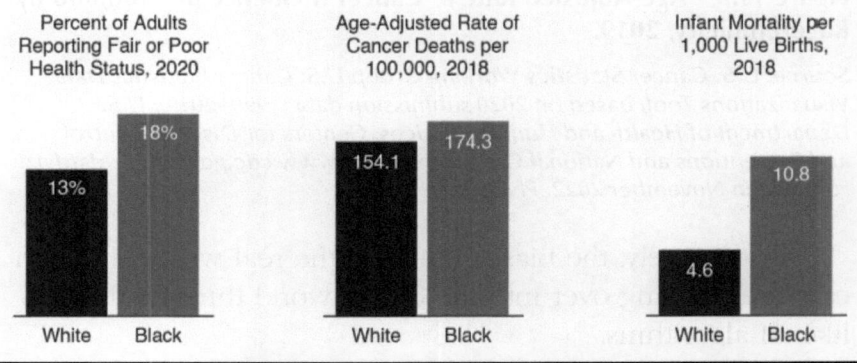

Figure 11.2   Black People Have Higher Rates of Illness and Death Compared to White People.

Source: Kaiser Family Foundation.

economic prosperity for the people impacted and the nation as a whole.

As noted in the previous chapter extensive, peer-reviewed studies of population health show that social determinants of health profoundly impact a wide range of health care outcomes.[10,11] Health disparities are created when financial stability, healthy food access, safe neighborhoods, health literacy, and quality education are lacking. This is true even within commercially insured populations (Figure 11.3 and 11.4).[12]

The Intelligent Health Revolution is opening doors to creating better health and well-being through a growing array of AI-driven, digital health solutions (more on this in Chapter 21). These new tools can potentially reduce many of the historical barriers to providing services.

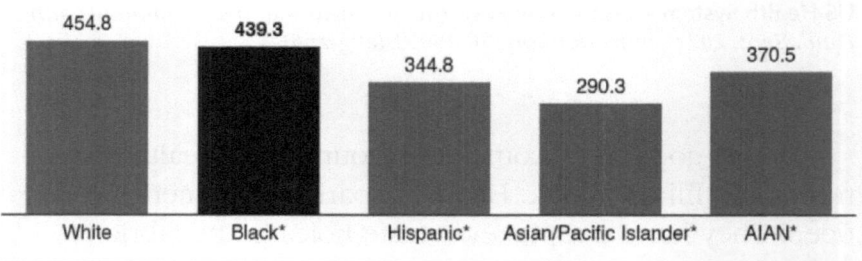

Figure 11.3   Age-Adjusted Rate of Cancer Incidence per 100,000 by Race/Ethnicity, 2019.

Source: U.S. Cancer Statistics Working Group U.S. Cancer Statistics Data Visualizations Tool, based on 2020 submission data (1999–2019): U.S. Department of Health and Human Services, Centers for Disease Control and Preventions and National Cancer Institute; www.cdc.gov/carcer/datdviz, released in November 2022. PNG

Unfortunately, the biases found in the real world of health care are crossing over into the digital world through things like AI algorithms.

In one case, a commercially available AI algorithm was used to assess which patients already undergoing medical treatments would graduate to receive additional specialized care.

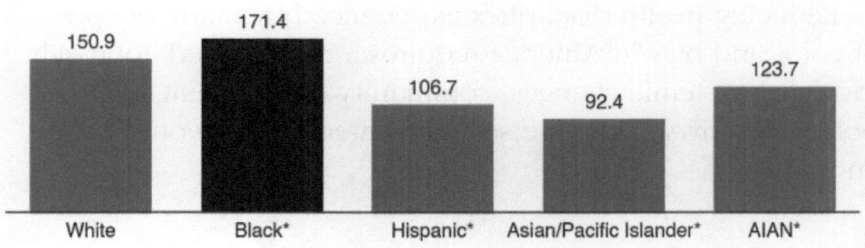

Figure 11.4   Age-Adjusted Rate of Cancer Deaths per 100,000 by Race/Ethnicity, 2019.

Source: U.S. Cancer Statistics Working Group U.S. Cancer Statistics Data Visualizations Tool, based on 2020 submission data (1999–2019): U.S. Department of Health and Human Services, Centers for Disease Control and Preventions and National Cancer Institute; www.cdc.gov/carcer/datdviz, released in November 2022. PNG

This widely used algorithm was four times more likely to recommend that White patients receive additional specialty care than Black patients, even though Black patients were often sicker.

This occurred because developers of the algorithm had correlated *health spending with health status*. This meant that a patient's past health expenditures became pivotal in predicting the risk of worsening health and the need for additional services. This was flawed logic as White Americans have had historically higher health expenditures than Black Americans *even when their health situations were identical.*

This algorithm was used over a million times to determine whether patients had access to additional care. Had it reflected accurate proportions of the sickest Black and White patients, 46% of Black patients would have been referred to more specialized care.[13]

Other studies have documented bias in algorithms used to guide the treatment of obstetrics, cardiology, oncology, and other specialties.[14]

Even climate change is not without bias. It impacts the health and well-being of all of us but has a greater impact on people of color.

Reducing health disparities experienced by many people of color and bias in America requires a multifaceted approach involving systemic changes, community engagement, and policy initiatives. Here are several strategies that would have an impact:

Investing in Public Health Infrastructure

Despite the many benefits of investing more in public health, our approach to it is similar to the break-fix model. We spend money to solve problems but invest little to prevent them from happening in the first place. It's a survive versus thrive model and mindset.

Investments in public health have largely come in response to major emergencies such as the pandemic. Once the immediate threat subsides, public health funding is reduced. This reactionary pattern leaves little room for investing and growing programs that produce measurable and sustainable health dividends.

Looking ahead, increased investments in a more substantial public health infrastructure gives us the opportunity to proactively address health issues caused by extreme weather-related events, the opioid epidemic, and infectious diseases which are emerging at an increasing rate. More on this in Chapter 19.

Reduce Poverty and Improve Economic Stability

Economic stability is critical to health. People who are not steadily employed are more likely to have poor health outcomes. Yet due to decades of marginalization, certain populations suffer from economic instability more than others.

Improving economic stability significantly diminishes health disparities. Poverty is intricately linked to limited access to health care services. Poor people often face barriers such as lack of health insurance, transportation issues, and inadequate health care facilities in their neighborhoods. Low-income families often struggle to afford nutritious food, leading to higher rates of obesity, malnutrition, and related health issues.

Financial instability, unemployment, and low incomes are associated with not only poor health outcomes but also reduced health care access and shorter life expectancies.

Investing in improved economic stability today has a downstream effect of breaking the cycle of poverty and poor health for future generations. One study notes that increasing a family's income with a child under five years old by just $3,000 a year can increase the child's adult earnings by as much as 20%.[15]

Improve Education Access and Quality

Education plays a pivotal role in shaping health outcomes and disparities. Access to quality education also enhances individual well-being and contributes to broader societal health equity.

Education is a determinant of socioeconomic status (SES), which influences health outcomes. Individuals with higher levels of education often have greater access to economic resources, including stable employment, health insurance, and housing. These resources, in turn, facilitate access to health care services, healthy food options, and opportunities for physical activity, all of which are critical for maintaining good health.

Education also plays a crucial role in shaping health behaviors and lifestyle choices. Higher levels of education are associated with increased health literacy, enabling individuals to make informed decisions about their health and navigate complex health care systems effectively.

Improve Health Care Access and Quality

Health care access and affordability are significant problems for many Americans, especially those with low incomes and people of color. Policymakers have the opportunity to expand access to health coverage, lower costs for care and treatment, and improve the quality of health care services.

A key issue and area of opportunity is eliminating what is known as the Medicaid coverage gap. This is where the income of an individual or family is too low to qualify for marketplace subsidies but too high to qualify for Medicaid coverage in their state, resulting in no affordable options for health coverage.

Those without access to affordable health insurance often delay or forgo necessary medical care, leading to worse health outcomes and higher health care costs in the long run.

The Medicaid coverage gap also strains health care providers and safety net organizations as they continue to serve uninsured patients who cannot afford to pay for medical services out-of-pocket. As discussed in Chapter 7, this can lead to financial challenges for hospitals, community health centers, and other health care providers, potentially compromising their ability to deliver quality care to all patients.

To eliminate these disparities and those that exist in economic and social systems, an intentional focus on addressing structural racism is critical. Improving the health of the most vulnerable populations will not only boost overall health outcomes and social well-being but also strengthen the economy and help to build a stronger, equitable future for all citizens.

For Your Consideration:

1. Has your understanding of health disparities changed after reading this chapter?
2. What is your view on structural racism? Do you believe that it exists and is in play when it comes to the health outcomes for certain populations of people?
3. Consider your access to health care, education, and economic opportunities. How might your experiences and access impact your health and longevity compared to others?
4. Reflect on the role of technology and AI in health care. How do you think biases in digital health tools, such as AI algorithms, could affect health care outcomes for different racial and ethnic groups?
5. Consider the broader implications of the historical and systemic factors contributing to health disparities. How can individuals and communities work together to address these issues?

Notes:

_____

_____

_____

_____

_____

_____

_____

_____

_____

_____

_____

_____

_____

_____

_____

_____

_____

_____

_____

_____

_____

_____

_____

_____

_____

_____

_____

_____

_____

_____

_____

Endnotes

1. Institute of Medicine (US) Committee on Understanding and Eliminating Racial and Ethnic Disparities in Health Care; Smedley BD, Stith AY, Nelson AR, editors. Unequal Treatment: Confronting Racial and Ethnic Disparities in Health Care. Washington (DC): National Academies Press (US); 2003. Executive Summary, https://www.ncbi.nlm.nih.gov/books/NBK220355/

2. Office of Minority Health Resource Center. "Profile: Black/African Americans", Black/African American – The Office of Minority Health, August 22, 2019, www.minorityhealth.hhs.gov/omh/browse.aspx?lvl=3&lvlid=61

3. Nambi Ndugga, Latoya Hill, and Samantha Artiga, Key Data on Health and Health Care by Race and Ethnicity, Kaiser Family Foundation, June 11, 2024, https://www.kff.org/racial-equity-and-health-policy/report/key-data-on-health-and-health-care-by-race-and-ethnicity/

4. Michelle Tong, Latoya Hill, and Samantha Artiga, Racial Disparities in Cancer Outcomes, Screening, and Treatment, February 3, 2022, https://www.kff.org/racial-equity-and-health-policy/issue-brief/racial-disparities-in-cancer-outcomes-screening-and-treatment/

5. Darren Liu, Hayley Schuchard, Betty Burston, Takashi Yamashita, and Steven Albert, Interventions to Reduce Healthcare Disparities in Cancer Screening Among Minority Adults: A Systematic Review. *Journal of Racial and Ethnic Health Disparities*, 8(1), May 15, 2020, 107–126, https://doi.org/10.1007/s40615-020-00763-1

6. Michelle Tong, Latoya Hill, and Samantha Artiga, Racial Disparities in Cancer Outcomes, Screening, and Treatment, February 3, 2022, https://www.kff.org/racial-equity-and-health-policy/issue-brief/racial-disparities-in-cancer-outcomes-screening-and-treatment/, 96.

7. Harvard T.H. Chan School of Public Health, Health Disparities Between Blacks and Whites Run Deep, 2016, https://www.hsph.harvard.edu/news/hsph-in-the-news/health-disparities-between-blacks-and-whites-run-deep/

8. Hispanic and Latino Health Disparities, Cigna, https://www.cigna.com/health-care-providers/resources/hispanic-and-latino-health-disparities

9. Zachary J. Ward, Michael W. Long, Stephen C. Resch, Catherine M. Giles, Angie L. Cradock, and Steven L. Gortmaker, Simulation of Growth Trajectories of Childhood Obesity into Adulthood. *New England Journal of Medicine,* 377, 2017, 2145–2153. https://doi.org/10.1056/NEJMoa1703860.

10. Hilary Graham and Piran CL White, Social Determinants and Lifestyles: Integrating Environmental and Public Health Perspectives. *Public Health*, 141, 2016, 270–278.

11. Lloyd I. Sederer, The Social Determinants of Mental Health. *Psychiatric Services*, 67(2), 2016, 234–235.

12. Megan F. Pera, Mary M. Cain, Ashleigh Emerick, Stephanie Katz, Nicole A. Hirsch, Bruce W. Sherman, and Dena M. Bravata, Social Determinants of Health Challenges Are Prevalent Among Commercially Insured Populations. *Journal of Primary Care & Community Health*, 12, 2021, 1–10.

13. Dissecting Racial Bias in an Algorithm Used to Manage the Health of Populations. *Science*, 366(6464), October 25, 2019, 447–453.

14. Darshali A. Vyas, Leo G. Eisenstein, and David S. Jones, Hidden in Plain Sight — Reconsidering the Use of Race Correction in Clinical Algorithms. *New England Journal of Medicine*, July 10, 2020, https://www.nejm.org/doi/full/10.1056/NEJMms2004740

15. Greg J. Duncan, Kathleen M. Ziol-Guest, and Ariel Kalil, Early-Childhood Poverty and Adult Attainment, Behavior, and Health. *Proceedings of the National Academy of Sciences* (PNAS), 2010.

THE AWAKENING

Your thoughts matter, but your actions matter more.

Scan me!

Scan this code for a message from the Author

Chapter 12

The Pandemic Showed Us That Change Is Possible

"It is not the strongest of the species that survives, nor the most intelligent that survives. It is the one, that is the most adaptable to change."

—*Charles Darwin*

It was early 2020 when COVID-19 came crashing into our lives without warning. The pandemic was simply there when the day before, it was not. We recognized it when our family, friends, and co-workers started getting sick and dying in numbers not seen since the beginning of the last century. Like something out of a bad science fiction movie, the humans versus virus battle was on.

Health care has always been steeped in emergency preparedness, but nothing prepared it for what was to come. ICUs were quickly overrun by critically ill patients. As COVID patients were highly infectious, treatments for other medical needs came to a grinding halt. The lack of everyday items

DOI: 10.4324/9781003600695-14

such as ventilators and personal protective equipment (PPE) became a matter of life and death.

Frontline caregivers worked around the clock. When systems were pressed to the brink, resourceful people stepped in to bolster, bridge, and fix what wasn't working. Makeshift ICUs' were created. Ventilators were MacGyvered back into service.

In the world of drug discovery, the race was on. As infection rates and death tolls climbed at a mind-blowing rate, we woke up to the fact that getting new drugs or a vaccine from the lab to the pharmacy historically took an average of 12 years at a cost of $2.6 billion.[1]

Almost overnight, consumers became legitimately fearful of premature death *en masse*. COVID cut to the core of what we universally care about the most. Our health. Our children. Our jobs and financial security. In a matter of weeks, this singular issue forced everyone to change their daily living activities and to see their life priorities in a different light.

The world was seemingly descending into darkness never seen by those walking the planet today. Just when it felt like the bad news would never end, something happened. As humans always do, we learned. We adapted. And we prevailed.

Never Let a Crisis Go to Waste—The Things We Learned

The pandemic challenged and changed all of us. It rearranged our priorities. Along the way it taught us valuable lessons. Most importantly, it showed us that when we pull together changing the way the health care system works is possible.

In the midst of the worst global health crisis in modern times we started a renaissance of new thinking and new approaches. We proved that an industry known for moving at glacial speed can move at warp speed when people are motivated and aligned with a common goal and purpose.

It wasn't easy, but it worked. Here's what we did differently:

Health leaders stepped up and demonstrated transformational leadership. Clinical, health, business, and elected leaders led from the front. They worked together to collaboratively and creatively develop new and novel approaches to solving problems.

From telehealth to expedited vaccine development, to remote work, leaders assessed long-standing work methods and quickly adapted to address the challenges before them.

Consumers adapted and took more control of their health. Without access to many traditional services, consumers used their home downtime to build bridges to managing their health needs.

With restrictions on in-person visits we tried new things like telehealth. We embraced digital health tools such as mobile health apps, wearable devices, and online portals to monitor our health, track symptoms, and manage chronic conditions remotely.

The pandemic prompted many of us to reevaluate the importance of health. More people began prioritizing preventive care and wellness activities to maintain overall health.

The pandemic accelerated a health movement that was already gaining traction. For example, the sale of Apple's health-app-infused smart watch surpassed the total number of watches sold by all Swiss watchmakers.[2]

A growing array of digital and AI tools became catalysts for change. We saw the benefit of leveraging our growing array of AI and digital technology capabilities. Humans fought and won the COVID battle. Artificial Intelligence (AI) was a primary weapon that allowed us to quickly turn the tide in our favor. It enabled and empowered clinicians and consumers alike to adapt at a much greater velocity.

Leaders and consumers rethought how to deliver care and services. Intelligent technologies were creatively put into service to make things smarter and faster.

Government Leaders enacted new legislative and regulatory measures to quickly adapt to the needs of the people and the health system. Guidelines and new funding for telehealth and other services were implemented to economically fuel new approaches to delivering health services.

Another important lesson the pandemic taught us was this: Humans often need a strong motive to change. Or as a mentor of mine from the South is fond of saying *"when people feel the heat, they see the light."*

In the early days of the pandemic everyone was motivated to change. The COVID crisis threatened our physical, mental and economic well-being. It gave us a universal challenge to face. It got us out of our comfort zones of doing nothing. We began taking control. We started thinking and acting differently.

In the end, it started a collective movement for change. The key to our success was that *everyone* played a role.

The pandemic was an abrupt wake-up call. But, unlike the COVID crisis which came roaring at us, the greatest health challenges we face today are quietly creeping into our lives day-by-day. Left unchecked they will be every bit as deadly and challenging as the pandemic.

We have an unprecedented opportunity to take what we've learned and make health care better for all. Let us use our newfound learnings to collectively create a new vision. To restore power to clinicians and consumers alike. To create a system that helps all citizens to be healthier while making better use of our human and financial resources.

Thomas Jefferson said, ***"Every generation needs a revolution."*** Let us take what we learned from fighting a global pandemic and apply it to improving the health of our people, our nation, and the planet.

For Your Consideration:

1. Did the pandemic change how you view your life's priorities? How did it affect your view of the importance of health?
2. Were there aspects of your health that you started to value more? Did the threats posed by the pandemic influence your overall outlook on life?
3. Consider the rapid advancements in health care and technology during the pandemic, such as telehealth and AI tools. What role do you see them playing in your future health management?
4. Did the pandemic change your view on how the healthcare system needs to change?
5. The chapter mentions the need for a collective movement for change. Do you agree? If yes, what steps are you willing to take to ensure that the lessons learned from the pandemic lead to lasting improvements in health and well-being?

Notes:

_____

_____

_____

_____

_____

_____

_____

_____

_____

_____

_____

Endnotes

1. FDA Drug Approval Process, Drug.com, April 13, 2020, https://www.drugs.com/fda-approval-process.html
2. Chris Wood, Apple Sold Nearly 10 Million More Watches Than the Entire Swiss Watch Industry in 2019—and It's a Sign the Wristwear Market Has Completely Changed. *Business Insider India*, February 6, 2020, https://www.businessinsider.in/tech/news/apple-sold-nearly-10-million-more-watches-than-the-entire-swiss-watch-industry-in-2019-and-its-a-sign-the-wristwear-market-has-completely-changed/articleshow/73985624.cms

Chapter 13

The Great Health Awakening

> "You may say I'm a dreamer. But I'm not the only one."
>
> —*John Lennon*

As a writer, I feel sorry for the word "epidemic" as it is often maligned and misunderstood. The clever folks who wrote the Merriam-Webster dictionary have come up with definitions for over 470,000 words. Here's what they tell us the word *epidemic* means:

> *"Affecting or tending to affect a disproportionately large number of individuals within a population, community, or region at the same time."*[1]

Now that we understand the true meaning of epidemic, I want you to imagine a remarkable transformation in the not-to-distant future that begins sweeping across the United States.

It's a ***wellness* epidemic** unlike any other. Just as the COVID-19 pandemic took the world by surprise, this movement starts out small (as epidemics always do) but quickly

DOI: 10.4324/9781003600695-15

becomes a seismic shift that reshapes the very fabric of our health system and society. It touches every citizen, community, and institution. It's a collective awakening that leaves *no one behind*.

What is the catalyst for this massive outbreak of health? The global pandemic that we all experienced. While our pandemic scars have faded, what lingers are the lessons we learned about how our health and well-being are interconnected to everything we hold dear.

And so, going forward *health and wellness* becomes contagious. These are no longer token topics used to sell gym memberships, fad diets, or the rhetoric of an archaic system that previously made money based on the volume of things done rather than the value they contributed to the health of individuals and a nation.

The health system of the future goes into a new orbit. It begins revolving around sustaining well-being rather than merely responding to illness.

Citizens who were once passive recipients of health care are now part of a system that actively embraces their needs. Everyone *has the opportunity* to leverage the system to become better stewards of their own health destiny.

Our talent pool of doctors, nurses, and health care professionals, who previously spent more time doing administrative work than working with patients and consumers, become members of the *keyboard liberation league*. They are freed from their keyboards and the labyrinth of administrivia that drained them of their passion. Their experience, energy, and wisdom are now unleashed to do the things that they dreamed of doing when they entered their profession.

America has become an exemplar for longevity. Living a long, healthy, and fulfilling life becomes less about winning the genetic lottery and more about the collective achievement of a system that recognizes the importance of having a healthy citizenry across *all stages of life*.

Businesses whose products and services were steadily losing their competitiveness in a global market because of the financial burdens of a bloated health system are riding a wave of productivity and innovation. They are cashing in on what comes to be known as America's wellness dividend. This dividend shifts more money from out-of-control benefit spending and into workers' take-home pay and better returns for shareholders.

Insurance companies and health plans meanwhile begin to report record financial returns that are pegged to a new business model which focuses on achieving standard health measures. After actuarial risk adjusting to include all populations, health plans do better financially when they demonstrate that those they cover are healthier than they would otherwise be.

Elected and government leaders who are consistently returned to office are those who step up to do the right things. They implement short- and long-range policies that promote health and social services that are inclusive of all citizens. They are beloved by voters and become known as the *"wellness warriors."*

The American view and definition of the "health system" evolves to focus on *"systems of health."* This broadens our definition of health and includes a more holistic approach to the environment, education, and food supply.

And so, right about now you are either rolling your eyes, or you are hearing the sound of our imaginary bubble POP.

But before you leave this vision consider this:

All revolutions start with a collective vision for what is possible.

Four Words That Changed the World

It was hotter than usual August in 1963 and the March on Washington for Jobs and Freedom was on. Dr. Martin Luther King Jr. had been asked to deliver a speech. At the time he was unknown to most Americans. This was about to change as all three major television networks were providing live coverage of the march.

The night before Dr. King gathered his advisors to seek advice about the next day's speech. His top aides cautioned him about using the familiar lines he typically used and instead urged him to use his "TV time" to outline a more practical approach by defining the platform and principles that Congress and the nation should consider.

After receiving suggestions from his staff, Dr. King retired to his room at the Willard Hotel in Washington, D.C., to finalize his speech.

History was made the following day. Had Dr. King followed the advice of his advisors he might have started his talk with *"I have a three-part plan on how to reduce the racial and economic disparities that exist in America today."*

Instead, he used four words that became the impetus for a revolution and a rallying cry that still rings in our ears as a symbol for what is possible:

I have a dream.

Dr. King's speech remains one of the most iconic moments in American history. It defined the Civil Rights Movement. It mobilized a nation. Ultimately, these four words led to the passage of the Civil Rights Act of 1964, which outlawed discrimination based on race, color, religion, sex, or national origin.

Dr. King and others, against all conventional wisdom and odds, had the courage and audacity *to dream.*

Changing Our Minds to Change the World

One of the most significant challenges in changing health care is that while everyone has complaints about the system, few have dreams of what it could be. Those who do have dreams of a better system often feel powerless. They don't know where to start.

Having a vision of a new system for health gives us a North Star. It gives us hope. It doesn't have to be a technicolor dream with all the details, but it should start with a sense of what could be.

If you are willing to dream of a better system for building healthy individuals, families, and a nation, turn the page. I want to tell you a little more about the health dividends that we can achieve if we choose to.

For Your Consideration:

1. Do you believe that the vision of the future outlined in this chapter is possible? Why or why not?
2. How would a nationwide *wellness epidemic* reshape your health habits and attitudes toward well-being? What steps could you take to be part of this collective movement for change?
3. What benefits or challenges do you foresee in embracing a system that prioritizes prevention over treatment? (Or at least raises our focus and investments in prevention to the same level as treatments?)
4. Do you believe achieving a "wellness dividend" is possible? If yes, what would it look like? How might it be measured?
5. What barriers would need to be addressed to move toward the vision described for America's future?

Notes:

_____

_____

_____

_____

_____

_____

_____

_____

_____

_____

_____

_____

_____

_____

Endnotes

1. Epidemic Definition & Meaning, Merriam-Webster, https://www.merriam-webster.com/dictionary/epidemic

Chapter 14

Achieving Health Dividends—The Economics of Health and Well-Being

"The best way to predict the future is to create it."

—Peter Drucker

As you consider creating your vision of what health care should be, a team of actuaries at Deloitte has conducted research on where health care could be going in the next two decades. Driven by new tech breakthroughs, changing consumer expectations and the unsustainable economics of the current system, their vision of health care's future is worth considering.

Their work suggests that by 2040 the center of gravity in U.S. health care will have shifted. Instead of continuing to perpetuate the existing break-fix model, the system will begin moving toward health spending that promotes health rather than merely treating sickness and delaying symptoms.

DOI: 10.4324/9781003600695-16

Investments in wellness, prevention, and early diagnoses could actually exceed treatment-based reactionary care.[1] This in turn, would empower and engage consumers to actively navigate their own health. In this case, "health" has been defined holistically as an overall state of well-being encompassing physical, mental, social, emotional, financial, and spiritual health.

Digital transformation, powered by shared data, secure platforms, and new technologies, would support the entire health system.

As this seismic shift occurs, it will impact the way health care is financed. The nation's health investment strategy would essentially flip with health and wellbeing activities accounting for nearly two thirds of spending (Figure 14.1).

If the Deloitte vision for the future sounds like a fantasy, consider this: The U.S. government estimates that health care spending could reach nearly $12 trillion by 2040 if nothing changes. This would mean that over a quarter of America's GDP would be spent on health care. Meanwhile the system's overall performance would stay the same or get worse.[2]

In contrast, Deloitte actuaries estimate that by investing in tools and systems that help people take an active role in their health, total health care spending could be reduced to $8.3 trillion. This $3.5 trillion *"well-being dividend"* would save money and also improve how the health system serves everyone in the country.[3]

Health and Economic Well-Being Is Cyclical

The relationship between health and economic well-being for individuals and nations is a cyclical thing. Healthier populations contribute to a stronger local and national economy. A stronger economy contributes to a healthier population.[4]

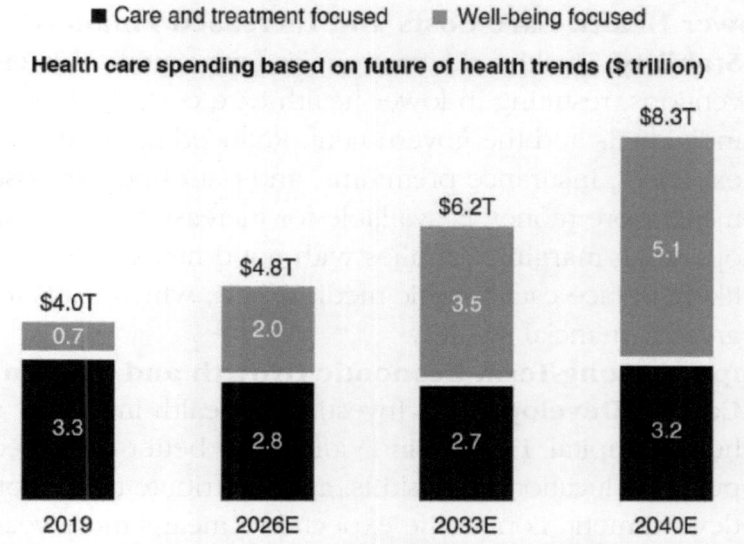

Figure 14.1 By 2040, Two-Thirds of Health Care Spending Will Likely Be on Well-Being and Early Detection of Diseases.
Source: Deloitte analysis. Breaking the Cost Curve.

The effects last throughout an individual's lifetime and actually produce measurable benefits for future generations.[5]

And so, just as the pandemic plunged us into one of the deepest economic contractions in decades, what would the impact be of a new health model that stimulates a major outbreak of health and wellness described in the last chapter?

The impetus for such change is already among us. Eighty-two percent of U.S. consumers consider wellness a top or important priority in their everyday lives.[6] The benefits of rethinking the health system to support the health aspirations of all Americans would:

Increase Productivity and Workforce Participation:
Healthy individuals are more likely to be productive. They experience fewer sick days, leading to increased labor force participation and overall productivity.

Lower Health Care Costs and Increased Financial Stability: Healthy citizens require fewer medical interventions, resulting in lower health care costs for both individuals and the government. Reduced medical expenses, insurance premiums, and out-of-pocket costs mean more money is available for increased salaries and operating margins. Families with good health are less likely to face catastrophic medical bills, which leads to greater financial stability.

Improve Long-Term Economic Growth and Human Capital Development: Investing in health improves human capital. Healthy individuals are better equipped to pursue education, gain skills, and contribute to economic development. Longer life expectancy means more years of productive work, savings, and investment. A healthier population can drive innovation, entrepreneurship, and technological advancements.

Research and evidence show that creating a "health dividend" is real and achievable. On average, healthier counties in the US have $3,734 higher per capita income, $5,302 higher average annual pay, $9,839 higher GDP per capita, and 0.6% lower unemployment rates.[7]

Let's apply these tenets with two important groups: Women and Millennials.

Women's Health and Economic Well-Being

Women are the bedrock of our economy and our communities. They make up nearly 60% of the paid U.S. workforce and 65% of the unpaid workforce of caregivers for children and other family members.[8]

Studies show that healthier women contribute to more productive and better educated communities.[9] Given their role in the economy, families and the community, women's health affects more than just them.

For many reasons women's health is a critical public health issue. Unfortunately, many aspects of the current health system diminish the ability of women to be healthy.

Even though women typically outlive men (greater lifespan) they spend 25% more time in "poor health" according to a study by the World Economic Forum and McKinsey and Company. On average, a woman will spend nine years in poor health. This affects her ability to be present and productive at home, in the workforce, and in the community. It also drags down the earning potential for women which further broadens existing income disparities.[10]

Why does this gap exist between women and men? Research suggests that this difference is mainly due to the structural and systemic barriers women face that are built into the current health system.

Research funding for women's health is often scarce. The National Institutes of Health (NIH) allocate just 11% of their total budgets to research that is health-specific to women.[11]

For example, despite women having a 50% higher mortality rate in the year following a heart attack, less than 5% of the NIH's budget for coronary artery disease supports women-focused research in this area.[12] Additionally, the analysis of data from one of the largest clinical trial registries in the world found that women represent less than 40% of the people enrolled in heart disease and stroke clinical research (Figure 14.2).[13]

Over the past ten years, there have been five times more scientific studies on erectile dysfunction than premenstrual syndrome.[14] In one trial where the medication sildenafil citrate was shown to relieve menstrual pain (the same compound that helps men get an erection), research was stopped due to a lack of funding.[15]

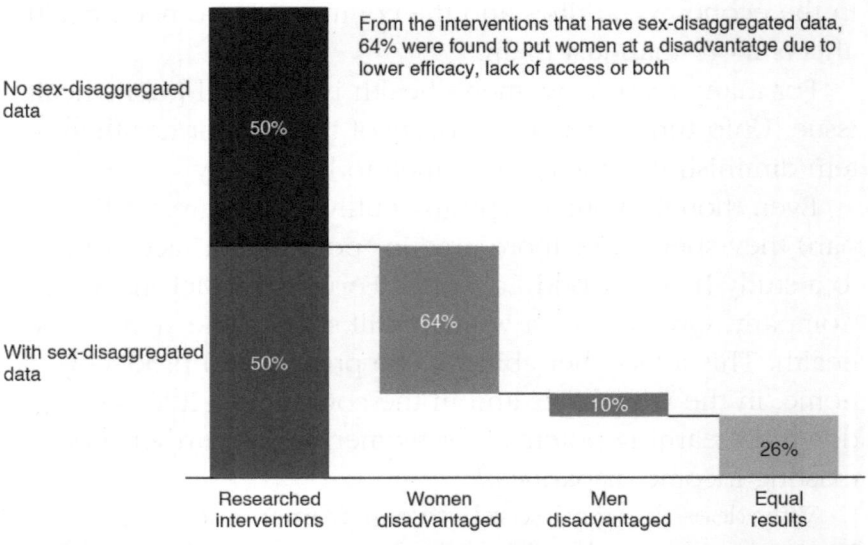

Figure 14.2   Effectiveness of and Access to Interventions between Men and Women.

Source: McKinsey Analysis, Closing the Women's Health Gap, https:// www.mckinsey.com/mhi/our-insights/closing-the-womens-health-gap-a-1- trillion-dollar-opportunity-to-improve-lives-and-economies

Over the past 20 years, women in the US have reported total adverse events from approved medicines 52% more frequently than men, and serious or fatal events 36% more frequently.[16] An analysis of all medicines withdrawn from the market for safety reasons since 1980 shows that products are 3.5 times more likely to be removed because of safety risks in women patients compared with men.

Analyses of U.S. health records and studies indicate that fewer than half of women living with endometriosis have a documented diagnosis.[17]

While such health disparities affect women from all age groups, 50% of the burden affects women of working age (Figure 14.3).

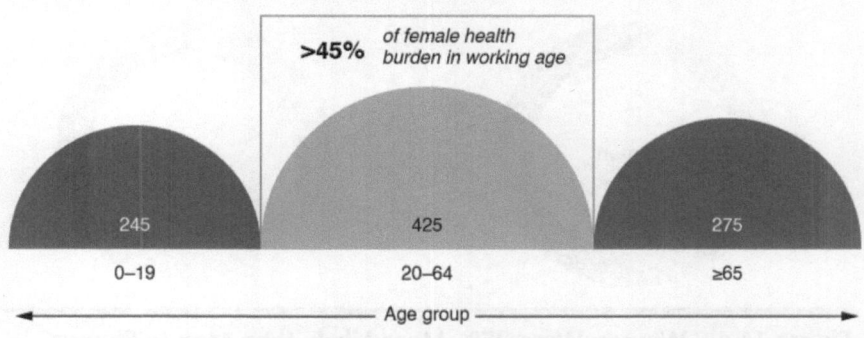

Figure 14.3   Almost Half of Health Burden Affects Women of Working Age.

Source: Global Burden of Disease Collaborative Network: Global Burden of Disease Study 2019 (GBD 2019), Institute for Health Metrics and Evaluation, 2022; McKinsey & Company.

[1]Disability-adjusted life years.

Decreasing the time women spend in poor health compared to men would improve the health and lives of millions of women and create a significant economic dividend.

The current women's health gap equates to 75 million years of life lost due to poor health or early death per year. That's the equivalent of seven days per woman per year (Figures 14.4 and 14.5).

Closing this gap would boost the global economy by at least $1 trillion annually by 2040. It would also allow women to add 1.7% to GDP. Equally important, closing this health gender gap would lift more women out of poverty and improve their ability to better provide for themselves and their families.

Investing in women's health shows a positive return on investment (ROI). For every $1 invested, approximately $3 is projected in economic growth.[18]

Have avoided care in the past year

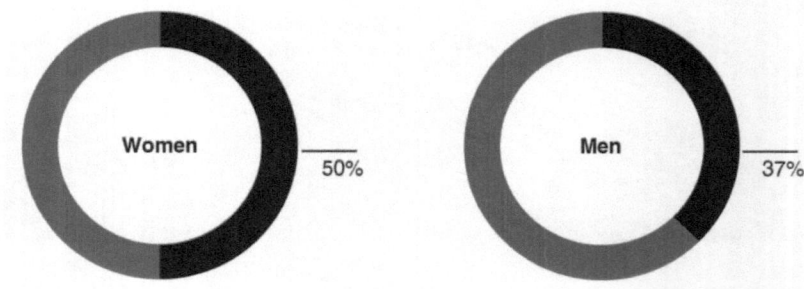

Figure 14.4 Women Were 35% More Likely than Men to Skip or Avoid Care.

Source: Deloitte Center for Health Solution' 2024 Health Care Consumer Survey; Deloitte Insights Deloitte.com/insights

Note: N = 2,003.

● Women ● Men

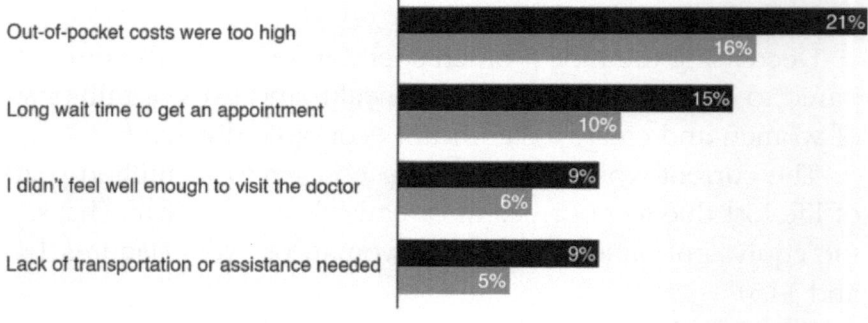

Figure 14.5 Out-of-Pocket Costs and Long Wait Times Are the Top Reasons Why Women Report They Are Skipping or Delaying Medical Care.

Source: Deloitte Insights Deloitte.com/insights.

Investing in Millennial Health

Millennials are the generation born between 1981 and 1996. They are the most educated, and connected generation the world has ever seen.[19,20]

Millennials now comprise the largest share of the U.S. population and labor force, placing them at the heart of U.S. economic growth as consumers, workers, and business owners. [21]

How their health plays out in the years ahead will determine not only the overall health of the country, but also its economic trajectory.

Unfortunately, the warning lights are beginning to blink. Millennials are showing signs of troubling generational health patterns that could hamper the future prosperity of millennials, and in turn the prosperity of society as a whole.

Data suggests that the health of millennials is declining faster than the previous generation as they age. This includes physical health conditions, such as hypertension and high cholesterol. It also includes behavioral health conditions, such as major depression (Figure 14.6).

CONDITION	GEN XERS (2014) (RATE PER 100)	MILLENNIALS (2017) (RATE PER 100)	DIFFERENCE IN PREVALENCE	
Major depression	4.7	5.6	18%	
Substance use disorder	1.6	1.8	12%	
Alcohol use disorder	1.5	1.5	0%	
Hypertension	12.5	13.7	10%	**MILLENNIALS VS. GEN XERS:** DATA SHOW **HIGHER PREVALENCE RATES AMONG MILLENNIALS** FOR 8 OF THE TOP 10 CONDITIONS
Hyperactivity	3.6	4.9	37%	
Psychotic conditions	0.6	0.5	–3%	
Crohn's disease/ Ulcerative colitis	1.2	1.3	15%	
High Cholesterol	10.8	12.6	7%	
Tobacco use disorder	6.5	7.2	11%	
Type II diabetes	3.4	4.1	19%	

Figure 14.6   Prevalence of Top 10 Conditions between Millennials and Gen Xers at the Same Age.

Source: The Health of Millennials, Blue Cross Blue Shield 2019.

If this trend plays out in its current trajectory, we will see an even greater demand for services in the years ahead. Under the most adverse scenario, millennial treatment costs could be 33% higher than what we've seen with Gen-Xers at a comparable age.

Even worse, millennials could feasibly see mortality rates climb more than 40% compared to Gen-Xers (those born between 1965 and 1979) at the same age.[22]

Poorer health among millennials will also keep them from contributing as much to the economy as they otherwise would. Under the most adverse set of projections, lower levels of health alone could cost millennials more than $4,500 per year in real per capita income compared to similarly aged Gen-Xers.[23]

Investing in a proactive model of services and care that can be personalized at the generational level can potentially change the course of generational health.

Creating a health dividend requires a fundamental shift in how we approach health care. By prioritizing wellness over sickness, we can build a system that reduces health care costs and improves the quality of life for all Americans. This approach can also be adjusted to be optimized for the unique needs of women and the health differences of each generation.

Policymakers, health care providers, and communities must collaborate to implement preventive care, promote holistic health, and invest in community-based programs. The benefits of such a transformation are clear: a healthier, more productive, and equitable society.

Now is the time to make this vision a reality.

For Your Consideration:

1. Do you believe that changing the model for health care delivery (as outlined in this chapter) would materially improve overall health and lower health care costs in America?
2. The chapter suggests that healthier populations contribute to a stronger economy, and vice versa. Do you agree?
3. Consider the data presented in this chapter on the health disparities between women and men. Why do you think differences exist? What should be done to close the gap?
4. The chapter highlights the potential impact of improving millennial health. How do you perceive the health challenges and opportunities facing your generation? What changes within health care would produce the best "health dividends" for you?
5. Envision a future healthcare system that fully embraces the shift toward holistic health and well-being. What aspects of your life would be positively impacted by this transformation?

Notes:

Endnotes

1. Future of Health Timeline, Deloitte US, https://www2.deloitte. com/us/en/pages/life-sciences-and-health-care/articles/ future-of-health-timeline.html
2. The $12 Trillion Question: What Will Health Spending Look Like in 2040?, Deloitte US, March 9, 2021, https://www2. deloitte.com/us/en/blog/health-care-blog/2021/the-12-trillion-dollar-question-what-will-health-spending-look-like-in-2040. html?icid=learn_more_content_click
3. The $12 Trillion Question: What Will Health Spending Look Like in 2040?, Deloitte US, March 9, 2021, https://www2. deloitte.com/us/en/blog/health-care-blog/2021/the-12-trillion-dollar-question-what-will-health-spending-look-like-in-2040. html?icid=learn_more_content_click.
4. Healthy Communities Mean a Better Economy, Blue Cross Blue Shield, 2017, https://www.bcbs.com/about-us/association-news/ blue-cross-blue-shield-association-report-finds-link-between-populations-health-and
5. Poverty Alleviation and the Economic Benefits of Investing in Health, Harvard T H Chan School of Public Health, April 11, 2016, https://www.hsph.harvard. edu/wp-content/uploads/sites/1496/2016/10/L-MLIH_ Health-economic-growth-and-development_ Atun-and-Kaberuka_4-11-16.pdf
6. The Top Wellness Trends in 2024, McKinsey & Company, January 16, 2024, The top wellness trends in 2024 | McKinsey
7. Healthy Communities Mean a Better Economy, Blue Cross Blue Shield, 2017, https://www.bcbs.com/about-us/association-news/ blue-cross-blue-shield-association-report-finds-link-between-populations-health-and, 113
8. Janet Foutty, Understanding the Impact of Women+ Health on Society. *Deloitte*, https://www2.deloitte.com/us/en/ pages/life-sciences-and-health-care/articles/impact-of-wom-ens-health-on-society.html
9. Kristine Husøy Onarheim, Johanne Helene Iversen, and David E. Bloom, Economic Benefits of Investing in Women's Health: A Systematic Review. *PLoS ONE*, 11(3), 2016, e0150120. https:// doi.org/10.1371/journal.pone.0150120

10. Kweilin Ellingrud, Lucy Pérez, Anouk Petersen, and Valentina Sartori, Closing the Women's Health Gap: A $1 Trillion Opportunity to Improve Lives and Economies, January 14, 2024, https://www.mckinsey.com/mhi/our-insights/closing-the-womens-health-gap-a-1-trillion-dollar-opportunity-to-improve-lives-and-economies?stcr=9066273D4332452B8FE6AF622116B7D4&cid=other-eml-ttn-mip-mck&hlkid=2c26322af88443c7a9fb52296115d760&hctky=14499108&hdpid=3348e329-704b-4ab8-8a7b-a4a6e8b5f370

11. Kweilin Ellingrud, Lucy Pérez, Anouk Petersen, and Valentina Sartori, Closing the Women's Health Gap: A $1 Trillion Opportunity to Improve Lives and Economies, January 14, 2024, https://www.mckinsey.com/mhi/our-insights/closing-the-womens-health-gap-a-1-trillion-dollar-opportunity-to-improve-lives-and-economies?stcr=9066273D4332452B8FE6AF622116B7D4&cid=other-eml-ttn-mip-mck&hlkid=2c26322af88443c7a9fb52296115d760&hctky=14499108&hdpid=3348e329-704b-4ab8-8a7b-a4a6e8b5f370

12. Elizabeth G. Nabel, Coronary Heart Disease in Women – An Ounce of Prevention. *New England Journal of Medicine*, 343, 2000, 572–574; Harvard Health Blog. Women and Pain: Disparities in Experience and Treatment, October 9, 2017: https://www.health.harvard.edu/blog/women-and-pain-disparities-in-experience-and-treatment-2017100912562.

13. Women Still Under Represented in Clinical Research, Science and Medicine That Could Save Them from Their No. 1 Killer, American Heart Association, February 2020, https://newsroom.heart.org/news/women-still-underrepresented-in-clinical-research-science-and-medicine-that-could-save-them-from-their-no-1-killer

14. Research Gate, Why Do We Still Not Know What Causes PMS?, 2016, https://www.researchgate.net/blog/why-do-we-still-not-know-what-causes-pms

15. R. Dmitrovic, A. R. Kunselman, and R. S. Legro., Sildenafil Citrate in the Treatment of Pain in Primary Dysmenorrhea: A Randomized Controlled Trial. *Human Reproduction*, 28(11), November 2013, 2958–2965, https://academic. oup.com/humrep/article/28/11/2958/628626; CBC, There's a Gender Gap in Medical Data, and It's Costing Women Their Lives, Says This Author. *CBC*, August 17, 2019, https://www.cbc.

ca/radio/thecurrent/the-current-for march-11-2019-1.5049277/
there-s-a-gender-
gap-in-medical-data-and-it-s-costing-women-their-lives-says-this
author-1.5049286

16. Ending the Neglect of Women's Health in Research. *British
Medical Journal*, 381, 2023, 1303, https://pubmed.ncbi.nlm.nih.
gov/37308180/.

17. World Health Organization, A Roadmap to Combat Postpartum
Haemorrh age Between 2023 and 2030, 2023, https:// cdn.
who.int/media/docs/default-source/reproductive-health/mater-
nal-health/pph-roadmap.pdf?sfvrsn=db36b511_3.

18. Closing the Women's Health Gap: A $1 Trillion Opportunity to
Improve Lives and Economies, World Economic Forum, January
2024, https://www.mckinsey.com/~/media/mckinsey/mckin-
sey%20health%20institute/our%20insights/closing%20the%20
womens%20health%20gap%20a%201%20trillion%20dollar%20
opportunity%20to%20improve%20lives%20and%20economies/
closing-the-womens-health-gap-report.pdf?shouldIndex=false

19. Michael Dimock, Defining Generations: Where Millennials End
and Generation Z Begins. *Pew Research Center*, January 17, 2019.

20. Michael Dimock, Defining Generations: Where Millennials End
and Generation Z Begins. *Pew Research Center*, January 17, 2019.

21. Michael Dimock, Defining Generations: Where Millennials End
and Generation Z Begins. *Pew Research Center*, January 17, 2019.

22. Blue Cross Blue Shield Association Study Finds Millennials
are Less Healthy than Generation X Were at the Same Age,
Blue Cross Blue Shield, April 24, 2019, https://www.bcbs.com/
about-us/association-news/blue-cross-blue-shield-association-
study-finds-millennials-are-less-healthy

23. Blue Cross Blue Shield Association Study Finds Millennials
are Less Healthy than Generation X Were at the Same Age,
Blue Cross Blue Shield, April 24, 2019, https://www.bcbs.com/
about-us/association-news/blue-cross-blue-shield-association-
study-finds-millennials-are-less-healthy

Chapter 15

Raising the Bar for Health Outcomes— The Happiness Factor

"Happiness is the highest form of health."

—*Dalai Lama*

As you contemplate your vision for what the American health care system should be and the health dividends that are important to you, I'd like to tell you a story about a small country with a big idea.

Sandwiched between the economic and political power-houses of China and India, is the Kingdom of Bhutan. While most nations strive for success, which is measured by things like gross domestic product (GDP), the elected leaders of Bhutan have an unconventional measure of national success. It's known as the Gross National Happiness Index (GNP).

The concept of pursuing the happiness of the citizens of Bhutan was implemented in 1972. Still, its origins go back to legal code from 1792 which states: *"The purpose of government*

 DOI: 10.4324/9781003600695-17

is to provide happiness to its people. If it cannot provide happiness, there is no reason for the government to exist."

Over the years, government leaders refined this philosophy and developed policies aimed at providing *enabling conditions* for citizens to pursue and achieve happiness.

Now consider this: Bhutan's Gross National Happiness concept is not dissimilar to the opening proclamation of America's Declaration of Independence which sets forth *"life, liberty and the pursuit of happiness"* as a founding principle.

The difference between what Thomas Jefferson penned in the summer of 1776 and the approach taken by Bhutan is that it defined conditions for happiness and put the health of its citizens at the center of a collective set of policies and actions that empower citizens to live their best lives.

Beyond definable health measures for its citizenry, Bhutan's overall assessment of well-being includes goals for sustainable and equitable socio-economic development, environmental conservation, preservation, and the promotion of culture.

Raising the Health Outcomes Bar

And so, what might we learn from a small kingdom that could be applied to defining a new approach to health and well-being in America?

It's something I call the *Happiness Factor.* Here's how it could work:

When asked to define the goal of our health system today, the answer most often given is to achieve some level of *health and well-being.*

If we state this goal as an equation it looks like this:

Health + Well-being = Achievement of the health system's goals.

Let's start with our definition of *health*. Look closely, and you will see that our answer to the "*health*" part of this equation in the current break-fix model focuses heavily on restoring something to a *former or original state*. If it's a joint replacement, it's returning to a normal range of movement. If it's cancer, it's the absence of cancer cells for a period of time.

For many serious medical conditions, achieving such outcomes is nothing short of a modern miracle that significantly impacts the quality of life.

So for now, let's consider the *"health"* portion of the system's goal as essential. It's the safety net that lays the foundation on which to build the next part of the equation which is *well-being*.

As we've already learned, today's health system is overweighted with restoring or fixing things. While important, this is different than the second part of the goal which is achieving and maintaining a state of *well-being*.

Merriam-Webster defines well-being as "the *state of being happy, healthy, or prosperous*."[1] Think about your experience with the pandemic, and chances are, you've had your own firsthand experience with the interrelatedness of happiness, health, and prosperity.

Creating a new vision for the health system allows us to rebalance the health *and* well-being equation. It provides the opportunity to reimagine outcomes and raise the bar on what we get out of the health system in the future.

Let's use the prevailing view of mental health services as an example of well-being. Everyone understands that the health system must be geared toward providing services for mental health (though it is often a lightning rod for what services are *actually* covered).

Once again, the current definition and expectations focus on the provision of services that mitigate or eliminate the presence of mental illness. And while this is an essential precursor to achieving well-being, it falls short of actually delivering on that goal.

Let's define the Happiness Factor as the ability to leverage and deploy new health models that help everyone move higher on the well-being scale.

It changes our expectations from the absence of medical and mental conditions that impede our health, to an approach and mindset that *helps people thrive.*

It raises the bar. Instead of mental health services that merely mitigate mental illness, it focuses on helping citizens achieve their best potential at all stages of life including while living with medical and mental health conditions.

If you are older, it helps close the gap between lifespan (the time you live) and healthspan (the quality of the time you have).

If you are younger, it seeks to optimize your current stage of life to not only increase your happiness factor today but increase your chances of being healthier and happier at future stages of your life.

The Happiness Factor is a conscious and purposeful move to challenge and change our expectations of what we get out of the health system. It raises the bar from being satisfied with the absence of disease or debilitating conditions to the greater presence of health and vitality that provides everyone with the opportunity to achieve higher levels of individual and collective well-being.

Think of this as a system that helps more people move toward living in the upper quadrant of a "well-being" continuum. It moves us away from activities that merely help us survive to an ecosystem that gives all citizens the opportunity to thrive.

For your Consideration:

1. Is happiness a condition for being healthy?
2. Is creating enabling conditions for happiness the responsibility of government? Why or why not?
3. Government leaders in Bhutan are charged developing policies and systems that create *enabling conditions* for citizens to pursue and achieve happiness. If such a goal were established for American leaders, would most Americans take advantage of such opportunities?
4. What are the most important elements that contribute to your own happiness and well-being?

Notes:

_____

_____

_____

_____

_____

_____

_____

_____

_____

_____

_____

_____

_____

_____

_____

_____

_____

_____

Endnote

1. Merriam Webster online dictionary, https://www.merriam-webster.com/dictionary/well-being.

Chapter 16

The Butterfly Effect Takes Flight

"Never doubt that a small group of thoughtful, committed citizens can change the world; indeed, it's the only thing that ever has."

—*Margaret Mead*

It was a wintery day in 1961 when Edward Lorenz, a mild-mannered meteorology professor at MIT, entered some numbers into a computer program simulating weather patterns and then left to get a cup of coffee while the machine ran. When he returned, he discovered something that would change the course of science.

Lorenz was experimenting to predict how small variations in things like temperature and wind speed might impact future weather patterns. He was repeating a simulation he'd run earlier, and almost by accident, rounded off one variable from 0.506127 to 0.506. To his surprise, that tiny alteration drastically transformed the whole pattern his program produced, over two months of simulated weather.

DOI: 10.4324/9781003600695-18

The unexpected result gave Lorenz a powerful insight into how nature works. Small changes can have large consequences. The idea came to be known as the *"butterfly effect"* after Lorenz suggested that the flap of a butterfly's wings might ultimately cause a tornado. (Math simulations have, in fact, proved that, under the right conditions, this could actually happen.)

From Lorenz's work came the founding principles of what we now know as "chaos theory." More importantly, it also reinforced how small changes can become the impetus for large-scale transformation in science and society.[1]

The Power of Small Actions

The Civil Rights Movement. The Berlin Wall. Brexit. These are examples of the Butterfly Effect. They demonstrate that each of us has the power to change things through small actions that collectively create movements that change history.

Movements begin with seemingly insignificant actions. Remember Rosa Parks? She wasn't trying to start a civil rights revolution when she refused to give up her bus seat. It is likely that she was simply tired and wanted to sit down. She was also probably frustrated and fed up with a system that ignored her needs and worked against her ability to live a good life.

Her small act of defiance was powerful. It sparked change. It spread from buses to lunch counters, showing that one small action can sometimeslead to a tidal wave of change.

Admittedly, the Butterfly Effect is inherently unpredictable. We don't know which action will be the one to tip the scales. But that's part of the magic. Embrace the uncertainty but recognize that small actions matter.

The Butterfly Effect is also a reminder of our power and our potential. It tells us that change doesn't always come from the top. It often starts from the bottom with ordinary people's small, seemingly insignificant actions.

As I noted in the first chapter, waiting for someone else to come along and fix health care has not worked. There is no one else. There is only us. There is only you.

And so, it's time to flap your wings. Try it. See what happens.

For Your Consideration:

1. Do you believe that small actions can have an impact on our world today?
2. Do you believe that there are actions you can take that would help to move health care in the right direction?
3. How often do you underestimate the power of your actions or words? What would you do differently if you believed that your small actions would make a big difference?
4. Reflecting on past movements and significant historical changes, how can we learn from these examples to bring about the changes we want to see?
5. Do you believe in the potential of a citizen-driven movement that can change the health care system? Why or why not?

Notes:

_____

_____

_____

_____

_____

_____

_____

_____

_____

_____

_____

_____

_____

Endnote

1. Peter Dizikes. When the Butterfly Effect Took Flight. *MIT News Magazine*, February 22, 2011, https://www.technologyreview.com/2011/02/22/196987/when-the-butterfly-effect-took-flight/

NEW BEGINNINGS

Scan me!

Scan this code for a message from the Author

Chapter 17

In Honor of Medical Misfits—The Art and Science of Thinking Differently

"Here's to the crazy ones. The misfits. The rebels.
The troublemakers. You can quote them, disagree
with them, glorify or vilify them. About the only
thing you can't do is ignore them."

—*Steve Jobs*

Had bumper stickers been in existence in the 1850s Dr. John
Snow would likely have sported one on the back of his car-
riage that was popular in the 1960s amongst the countercul-
ture crowd that read:

Subvert the Dominant Paradigm.

It was 1854 and a deadly outbreak of cholera was raging
through London. At the time, the city's leading physicians and

scientists believed the disease traveled in a miasma—a floating cloud of sickness.

Enter Dr. John Snow, an unknown, upstart physician who also lived in the neighborhood that was at the epicenter of the outbreak. Watching his neighbors die en-masse, Snow had a different view. He believed the root cause of the outbreak was not bad air but contaminated water that was transmitting the disease.

When Snow presented his theory and supporting work to London's medical leaders he was rebuffed. But he persevered and through a mix of personal interviews, clever detective work, and data analysis that included tables and a famous map, Snow managed to stop the outbreak and convince local public health officials that cholera could be transmitted through water, not a miasma. His work ushered in a new medical specialty we now call epidemiology (the science/study of diseases and disorders affecting populations of people).

Fast forward to the 1970s. Even in the face of compelling evidence, the introduction of new technology for minimally invasive surgical procedures (endoscopy) was met with resistance in the surgical community.

Leading surgeons at the time saw little use for "key-hole" surgery as the prevailing view and practice was that *large medical problems required large incisions."* Today, the endoscopic revolution is seen as one of the most significant breakthroughs in contemporary medical history.[1]

Health Care Has Been Here Before—Change Is Hard

Ever since medicine came out of the shadows and into the light as a data-driven, scientific discipline, we've aspired to be better. Medical advancements such as vaccines, antibiotics, and other breakthroughs have played a crucial role in reducing the impact of infectious diseases and improving overall health.

Public health initiatives have led to better sanitation measures, clean water supplies, and waste disposal systems that significantly reduce environmental health risks. Health education efforts are empowering citizens by increasing awareness of healthy lifestyle choices and preventive measures that improve health and longevity.

Standing behind every significant advancement that made the world a healthier place were innovation leaders who demonstrated two qualities that set them apart from their traditional-thinking counterparts.

First, change-makers view the problems they are trying to solve with a different lens compared to others. They *think differently.*

Second, not only do they think differently, but they are also willing to *challenge the status quo* in their quest to make health care better. They stand as exemplars for something often missed by others which is:

No one ever changed the world by doing more of the same thing.

In making this statement, let me be clear: If you are a surgeon, I am not suggesting you go into the operating room and announce to your patients and team that you are going to try freestyling.

There is a historical, evidence-driven order in many aspects of medicine including *proven clinical best practices* that lead to repeatable quality outcomes. We must honor time-tested, data-driven best practices *while thinking differently about how we apply the science of medicine and public health to measurably improve health outcomes, to be more inclusive and more efficient in using of our finite resources.*

The Art and Science of Thinking Differently

Steve Jobs was a genius-level innovator who made *"thinking differently"* cool. He drove Apple's now-famous *"Think Different"* advertising campaign to inspire consumers and the company's innovation efforts. The campaign reminded consumers, and employees alike, that the *"crazy ones...see things differently."*

True innovators excel at thinking differently. They connect the unconnected. They engage in associational thinking by taking a little bit of this and then sprinkling it in with little bit of that to churn out new solutions that slingshot ahead of their traditional-thinking counterparts.

They approach old problems in new ways. Often, their goal is not to play a better game but to change the game itself.

Innovation Leaders Are Not Equal

While most health leaders like to think of themselves as innovators, research and history show that some have either never been good at thinking differently or that they, over time, lost their ability to think differently.

Why? It's not that our genetic code automatically shuts it down at a certain age. Instead, many of us grew up, or have worked in environments where thinking differently was punished instead of praised.

For example, telehealth/telemedicine existed for three decades before the onset of the COVID-19 pandemic. Research and experience demonstrated many times over that it was clinically efficacious and cost-effective. It was also a very convenient option for certain types of cases with patients and health consumers.

And so, why did it take a global pandemic to pull this forward for the world to see and use?

Research shows that there are differences between those who innovate and those who *only think about innovating*.

Successful innovators spend 50% more time trying to think differently than non-innovators. In other words, non-innovators do occasionally think differently but not as often as true innovators.[2]

Thinking differently is hard for some. Researchers at Harvard Medical School report that 60% to 80% of adults find thinking differently uncomfortable. Some find it exhausting.[3]

The good news is that no one has a corner on thinking differently. It is estimated that one-third of our innovation capacity comes from how we are wired genetically with two-thirds being driven by our environment. A study of over 5,000 entrepreneurs and executives shows that almost anyone who consistently makes the effort can think differently.[4]

If adults practice things like associational thinking long enough, the task of thinking differently no longer exhausts but energizes them. Like most skill-based activities, if we slog away at it and practice over time, the task becomes easier. And that's when the most creative ideas pop out.

The impact of thinking differently is not always instantaneous. When a young Alexander Graham Bell invented the telephone, early ideas for its use included using the phone to alert customers that a message had been received at the telegraph office.[5]

We are living in a time of unbelievable, indescribable, and unpredictable change. What is good enough today will be out-of-date tomorrow.

Leaders who are self-satisfied and complacent with how health care works today will be eclipsed by those who think differently, plan creatively, and act innovatively to further the collective mission of better health for all.

True innovators are a special breed. They think differently. They challenge the traditional point of view. They take on maintaining the status quo to push for something better.

Here's to the misfits. Whether a clinician, consumer, or politician, may you come forward with *your* ideas for positive change.

For Your Consideration:

1. What are your thoughts on how innovating health care will require us to think and act differently?
2. Have you experienced people in your work or personal life that were great examples of innovators who thought differently?
3. Do you have ideas that might seem unconventional that might make health care better? Explain your idea to someone else.

Notes:

_____

_____

_____

_____

_____

_____

_____

_____

_____

_____

_____

_____

_____

_____

_____

_____

_____

_____

_____

_____

Endnotes

1. Grzegorz S. Litynski. Endoscopic Surgery: The History, the Pioneers. *World Journal of Surgery*, 23(8), 1999, 745–753. https://doi.org/10.1007/s002689900576.PMID: 10415199
2. Jeff Dyer, Hal Gregersen, et al., *The Innovator's DNA, Updated, with a New Preface: Mastering the Five Skills of Disruptive Innovators*. Harvard Business Review Press, 2019.
3. Shelley Carson, *Your Creative Brain: Seven Steps to Maximize Imagination, Productivity, and Innovation in Your Life*. Harvard Business Review Press, 2010.
4. Jeff Dyer, *The Innovator's DNA, Updated, with a New Preface: Mastering the Five Skills of Disruptive Innovators*. Harvard Business Review Press, 2019.
5. Tom Wheeler, *Techlash – Who Makes the Rules in the Digital Gilded Age*. Brookings Institution Press, 2023, p. 33.

Chapter 18

Let's Stop Wounding Our Heroes

"Your profession is not what brings home your paycheck. Your profession is what you were put on Earth to do with such passion and such intensity that it becomes spiritual in calling."

—*Vincent Van Gogh*

Of all the lessons learned from fighting a pandemic, none was more frightening or important than discovering how dependent the system is on how we treat our doctors, nurses, and frontline caregivers.

They were already in short supply with burnout on the rise when the pandemic hit. As multiple waves of COVID variants washed over us, frontline health workers stepped in at great risk and made personal sacrifices to care for highly infectious patients.

From pop-up ICUs to work-arounds to bridge shortages of ventilators and supplies, front-line medical workers kept the system afloat using their skills, experience, and ingenuity.

They witnessed and managed patients' pain, suffering, and mortality at a rate not seen in a century. Some witnessed more

DOI: 10.4324/9781003600695-21

deaths on a double shift than they did in a normal year. They delivered the bad news to families and managed end-of-life care. They were often the last face and warm voice a COVID victim saw and heard.

In the end, they not only saved lives, but they saved the system from total collapse.

In exchange for their tremendous dedication and sacrifices, we expressed our gratitude. We called them *heroes*. And we *PROMISED* to do better in how we treated them once the COVID crisis passed.

Promises made should be promises kept. While we continue to talk about workforce burnout using polite terms with concern in our voices let us be clear:

> *A system with a charter of healing continues to harm in record numbers the very people in short supply who are there to take care of the rest of us. Despite our gratitude and promises made, the burnout felt by our nurses, doctors, and other frontline health workers is worse today than it's ever been.*

Burnout is on the rise. Significantly more nurses and other health care workers are reporting burnout today than during the pandemic according to a study by the Centers for Disease Control and Prevention (CDC).[1]

- Fifty-five percent of front-line health care workers report burnout with the highest rate (69%) among the youngest staff.[2]
- Half of nurses report feeling emotionally drained (50.8%), used up (56.4%), fatigued (49.7%), burned out (45.1%), or at the end of the rope (29.4%) "a few times a week" or "every day."[3]

- Twenty-five percent of nurse leaders report not being emotionally healthy.[4]
- Nearly two-thirds of doctors are experiencing at least one symptom of burnout, a massive increase from before the pandemic.[5]

Burnout isn't just another new buzzword. It's well-defined in medical literature. The Maslach Burnout Inventory, first published in 1981, measures burnout on three dimensions: emotional exhaustion, depersonalization from work, and a sense of personal accomplishment (Figure 18.1).[6]

And while the idea of burnout has become almost ubiquitous across all industries today, its impact in health care is hazardous to everyone's health.

For front-line health workers burnout is linked to higher rates of depression, alcohol abuse, suicidal ideation, cardiovascular diseases, sleep disturbances, and more.[7]

Burnout among our health workers is also linked to *harming patients*. It increases medical errors and worsens patient outcomes.

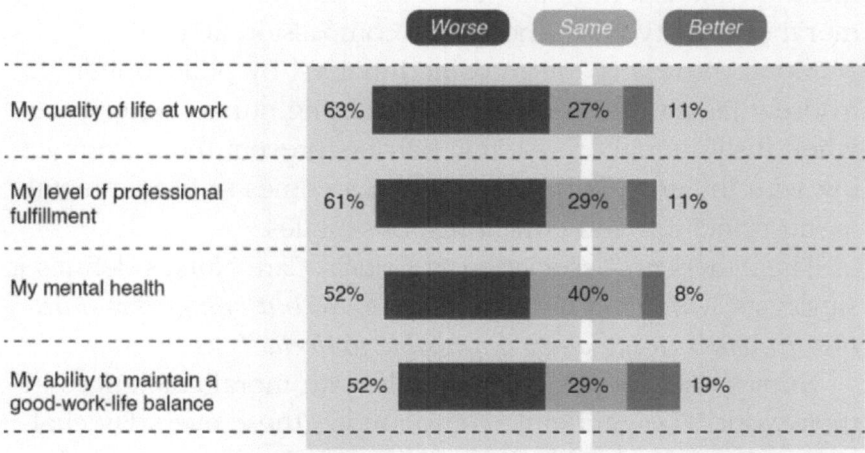

Figure 18.1 Physicians Comparing Before the Pandemic to Now.

Source: MD Analytics Survey 2023.

- Major medical errors reported by surgeons are strongly related to their degree of burnout and their mental quality of life.[8]
- Physicians reporting one or more conditions of burnout are significantly more likely to deliver lower-quality of care and have lower patient satisfaction ratings.[9]

Clinician burnout is a symptom of deeper issues for those forced to work in a broken system. This *"brokenness"* includes excessive administrative burdens, workplace chaos, endless reporting requirements, and organizational cultures that foster lack of connectedness, reduced control, diminished meaning in work, and a fundamental lack of trust.[10]

Burnout Is a Symptom of a Deeper Issue

Burnout is one of many symptoms seen in those experiencing a condition known as *moral distress*.[11] Other symptoms include exhaustion, numbness, disconnection, and diminished moral sensitivity (also known as "compassion fatigue").

Moral distress is a term coined in 1984 by philosopher Andrew Jameton to describe the suffering nurses experience when institutional or systemic barriers prevent them from acting with integrity, particularly when it comes to fundamental moral principles and ethical responsibilities.[12]

The American Association of Critical Care Nurses defines it simply as *"knowing the right thing to do but being in a situation in which it is nearly impossible to do it."*[13]

Nurses and doctors wrestle daily with moral challenges in their work. The pandemic compounded these everyday challenges. Frontline health workers struggled to maintain their professional, emotional, and moral equilibrium when caught in tragic situations beyond their control. And while the pandemic has passed and the issues are different, doctors, nurses, and others are still struggling.

The most damaging aspect of moral distress is instilling in our health experts an overwhelming sense of powerlessness. It's when they are put in a position where they feel they have to compromise themselves, or something they hold dear due to external forces that are beyond their control.

It's also the sense of frustration that others don't see or grasp a moral imperative that is clear to them.

Psychologists tell us that humans manage such stress in one of three ways: fight (try to regain control), flight (disengaging by quitting), and freeze (going through the motions and dissociation).

Frontline health care workers at all levels are increasingly burned out, overworked, and unsatisfied. They're walking out in droves to explore new opportunities or exiting the workforce altogether.

- During the COVID-19 pandemic, 100,000 registered nurses (RNs) left the workforce due to stress, burnout, and retirements.
- By 2027, almost 900,000, or about one-fifth of registered nurses, intend to leave the workforce.[14]
- One in five physicians surveyed during the pandemic said they planned to leave medicine within the next two years, while one in three said they'd cut back on their hours.

The Coming Care Calamity If Nothing Changes

Health care today employs more people than any other industry in the US including manufacturing and retail. One out of every eight workers toil in the field of health. That's 16 million workers and growing. A third of all new jobs created in this decade will be in health care.[15][16]

And while these numbers are impressive, we are nowhere close to having enough qualified health workers to keep up with today's demand, let alone for what is coming. At least not the way the health system operates today.

- Eighty-three million people in the US currently live in areas without sufficient access to a primary care physician.[17]
- More than one-third of Black Americans live in cardiology deserts.
- Nearly half of all practicing physicians in the US today are over age 55. It takes a decade or more to educate and train a physician.[18]

America will face a shortage of up to 124,000 physicians by 2033 and will need to hire at least 200,000 nurses per year to meet increased demand and to replace retiring nurses.[19]

The issue is not just a shortage of physicians and nurses. We'll likely see a shortage across all job categories of up to 3.2 million health care workers by 2026.[20]

The current workforce shortages, combined with an aging population, and a rise in chronic diseases and behavioral health conditions, have America on a collision course with disaster.[21]

Change Is Needed Now

Chronic burnout is a leading indicator that clinicians' jobs are unsustainable. The industry and Americans cannot continue to accept the status quo.

Organizational and systemic factors, including work design, culture, workforce supply, and policy are major contributors to worker burnout, which, in turn, leads to worker shortages.

The good news is that all these things are within our control to change.

Stabilizing the health care talent crisis starts with redesigning the health system, investing in people, and creating sustainable policies that rebuild trust in leadership.

The building blocks for such transformation include:

Restoring trust in organizational leadership. A survey by Deloitte notes that fewer than half (45%) of frontline clinicians trust their organization's leadership to do what's right for its patients. Even fewer, 23%, trust their leadership to do what's right for workers. These two types of trust—to do right by patients and to do right by workers—are highly correlated and associated with significantly lower clinician burnout.[22]

Reimagining care delivery and redesigning the work. Related to restoring leadership trust, clinicians in this Deloitte survey gave their organizations a grade of "C–" for their efforts to address burnout. The respondents identified many unnecessary and low-value tasks that take time away from patient care, such as those that satisfy administrative requirements (32%) and work that could be done by others or automated (20%). Yet, they have low expectations of their organizations to innovate.[23]

The path forward involves a complete care model transformation and job redesign.

Investing in technology: Many doctors currently spend more time entering data into Electronic Health Record systems (EHR) than they spend with their patients.[24] More than 70% say the use of antiquated EHRs has increased the number of hours worked and contributes to physician burnout.[25]

A study by McKinsey & Company concluded that using AI and intelligent solutions in health care could reduce repetitive activities performed by clinicians by 36%.[26]

Imagine eliminating a third of lower-value, repetitive activities that doctors, nurses, and others deal with every day.

Rethinking where care is delivered. As more care moves out of hospitals and into outpatient and other alternative sites of care, including telehealth and digital services there is the opportunity to rethink and redesign clinical workflows that reduce or eliminate the low-value, repetitive activities that wastes time for clinicians and keeps them from practicing at a higher level.

Redesigning work teams. Implement comprehensive interdisciplinary care teams that take advantage of team members' strengths, bring in more assistive clinical workers, and allow everybody to operate at the top of their license.[27]

Burnout is not just an individual struggle. It's a crisis that impacts the quality of care we all receive, the sustainability of the health care workforce, and the overall effectiveness of the health care system. As a society, we owe it to those who care for us to create an environment where they can thrive, both professionally and personally.

For Your Consideration:

1. If you are a health professional have you experienced signs of burnout? How has this affected your work and your feelings about yourself and your profession?
2. If you are a patient or health consumer, have you been impacted by the growing shortage of clinicians or seen signs of burnout in the medical professionals you have interacted with?
3. How do you see burnout affecting the quality of care patients receive?
4. Reflect on the idea that burnout is rooted in systemic issues such as administrative burdens, lack of control, and inadequate support. What changes are necessary to address burnout effectively?

Notes:

Endnotes

1. *Vital Signs:* Health Worker–Perceived Working Conditions and Symptoms of Poor Mental Health — Quality of Worklife Survey, United States, 2018–2022. *CDC Morbidity and Mortality Weekly Report,* Octobert 24, 2023, https://www.cdc.gov/mmwr/volumes/72/wr/mm7244e1.htm

2. Retention Requires Reimaging Work and the Work Experience, Deloitte, https://www2.deloitte.com/us/en/pages/life-sciences-and-health-care/solutions/workforce-retention-reimagine-reengagement.html

3. NCSBN Research Projects Significant Nursing Workforce Shortages and Crisis, NCSBN, April 23, 2023, https://www.ncsbn.org/news/ncsbn-research-projects-significant-nursing-workforce-shortages-and-crisis

4. Nurse Leaders' Top Challenges, Emotional Health, and Areas of Needed Support, July 2020 to August 2021, Association of Nurse Leaders, August 2021. https://www.aonl.org/resources/nursing-leadership-covid-19-survey

5. Oliver Whang, Physician Burnout Has Reached Distressing Levels, New Research Finds. *The New York Times,* September 29, 2022, https://www.nytimes.com/2022/09/29/health/doctor-burnout-pandemic.html#

6. Oliver Whang, Physician Burnout Has Reached Distressing Levels, New Research Finds. *The New York Times,* September 29, 2022, https://www.nytimes.com/2022/09/29/health/doctor-burnout-pandemic.html#

7. Shanafelt, Tait D et al., The Well-Being of Physicians. *The American Journal of Medicine,* 114(6), 513–519, https://www.amjmed.com/article/S0002-9343(03)00117-7/abstract

8. Tait D. Shanafelt, Charles M. Balch, Gerald Bechamps, Tom Russell, Lotte Dyrbye, Daniel Satele, Paul Collicott, Paul J. Novotny, Jeff Sloan, and Julie Freischlag. Burnout and Medical Errors Among American Surgeons. *Annals of Surgery,* 251(6), June 2010, 995–1000. http://dx.doi.org/10.1097/SLA.0b013e3181bfdab3. PMID: 19934755. https://pubmed.ncbi.nlm.nih.gov/19934755/

9. Carolyn S Dewa et al., The Relationship Between Physician Burnout and Quality of Healthcare in Terms of Safety and Acceptability: A Systematic Review, https://bmjopen.bmj.com/content/7/6/e015141

10. Practice Transformation: Measure, American Medical Association, February 13, 2024, https://www.ama-assn.org/practice-management/sustainability/practice-transformation-measure

11. Samantha Stein Psy.D., That Powerlessness You Feel Is Called "Moral Distress". *Psychology Today,* March 16, 2021, https://www.psychologytoday.com/us/blog/what-the-wild-things-are/202103/powerlessness-you-feel-is-called-moral-distress

12. Samantha Stein Psy.D., That Powerlessness You Feel Is Called "Moral Distress". *Psychology Today*, March 16, 2021, https://www.psychologytoday.com/us/blog/what-the-wild-things-are/202103/powerlessness-you-feel-is-called-moral-distress

13. AACN Position Statement: Moral Distress in Times of Crisis, American Association of Critical Care Nurses, March 1, 2020, https://www.aacn.org/policy-and-advocacy/aacn-position-statement-moral-distress-in-times-of-crisis

14. NCSBN Research Projects Significant Nursing Workforce Shortages and Crisis, NCSBN, April 13, 2023, https://www.ncsbn.org/news/ncsbn-research-projects-significant-nursing-workforce-shortages-and-crisis

15. Derek Thomson, Health Care Just Became the U.S.'s Largest Employer. *The Atlantic*, 2018, https://www.theatlantic.com/business/archive/2018/01/health-care-america-jobs/550079/

16. Derek Thomson, Health Care Just Became the U.S.'s Largest Employer. *The Atlantic,* 2018, https://www.theatlantic.com/business/archive/2018/01/health-care-america-jobs/550079/

17. American Medical Association. Practice Transformation: Measure, February 13, 2024.

18. AMA President Sounds Alarm on National Physician Shortage, American Medical Association, October 25, 2023, https://www.ama-assn.org/press-center/press-releases/ama-president-sounds-alarm-national-physician-shortage

19. Jacqueline Renfrow, AAMC Estimates 124K More Physicians Will Be Needed by 2034, with the Largest Gap Among Specialists, Fierce Healthcare, June 15, 2021, https://www.fierce-healthcare.com/practices/physician-shortage-continues-to-widen-now-estimated-at-124-000-by-2034

20. Fact Sheet: Strengthening the Health Care Workforce, The American Hospital Association, https://www.aha.org/fact-sheets/2021-05-26-fact-sheet-strengthening-health-care-workforce

21. Fact Sheet: Strengthening the Health Care Workforce, The American Hospital Association, https://www.aha.org/fact-sheets/2021-05-26-fact-sheet-strengthening-health-care-workforce

22. Addressing Health Care's Talent Emergency, Deloitte, November 15, 2022, https://www2.deloitte.com/us/en/insights/industry/health-care/healthcare-workforce-shortage-solutions.html

23. Addressing Health Care's Talent Emergency, Deloitte, November 15, 2022, https://www2.deloitte.com/us/en/insights/industry/health-care/healthcare-workforce-shortage-solutions.html

24. How Doctors Feel About Electronic Health Records National Physician Poll, Stanford University and the Harris Poll. 2018, Stanford, https://med.stanford.edu/content/dam/sm/ehr/documents/EHR-Poll-Presentation.pdf

25. How Doctors Feel About Electronic Health Records National Physician Poll, Stanford University and the Harris Poll. 2018, Stanford, https://med.stanford.edu/content/dam/sm/ehr/documents/EHR-Poll-Presentation.pdf

26. Michael Chui, Where Machines Could Replace Humans-And where They Can't, McKinsey & Company, 2017, https://www.mckinsey.com/business-functions/digital-mckinsey/our-insights/where-machines-could-replace-humans-and-where-they-cant-yet

27. Howard Drenth, Evolving the Team-Based Care Model, Deloitte, September 8, 2022, https://www2.deloitte.com/us/en/insights/industry/health-care/team-based-care.html

Chapter 19

Healthy People Require a Healthy Planet

"Together we shall save our planet. Save it we can. Save it we must."

—*John F. Kennedy*

Hidden in the shadows of our bustling cities and vast landscapes lurks a silent health crisis. It's found in the air we breathe and the water we drink. Climate change once evoked images of melting ice caps and stranded polar bears. It's now worked its way into the most intimate aspects of our lives. It's a burden on your health now. It will be a bigger burden on your children's health if we do nothing.

Regardless of your view on climate change, the physical environment you and your family live in is one of the single most important determinants of health.

It's not like this is a new discovery. Hippocrates wrote the essay *"Air, Water and Places"* in 400 BCE to shine a light on the connections between our health and the environment.[1] With 2,000 years' advance notice, you would think we humans would have done a better job of getting this right.

DOI: 10.4324/9781003600695-22

Today we are increasingly coming to terms with the reality that the planet which sustains all of us has very thin skin.

The World Health Organization calls climate change the greatest health threat facing humanity today.[2] Twenty-four percent of all deaths globally are in some ways attributable to environmental factors.[3]

Climate change is expected to significantly impact human health and death rates over the next 20 years. The effects will be wide-ranging, affecting various aspects of health through direct and indirect pathways.

Here are some of the significant health impacts we face:

Increase in Heat-Related Illnesses and Deaths

As global temperatures rise, the frequency, intensity, and duration of heatwaves are expected to increase. Extreme heat can lead to heat exhaustion, heatstroke, and worsening of cardiovascular and respiratory conditions. Vulnerable populations, such as the elderly, children, and those with pre-existing health conditions, are at greater risk.

As I write this, multiple sources are confirming that 2023 was the hottest year on record. This trend continued into 2024, with the summer of 2024 being the hottest ever recorded.[4]

Worsening Air Quality

Higher temperatures increase the formation of ground-level ozone, a major component of smog. This can worsen respiratory diseases like asthma and chronic obstructive pulmonary disease (COPD). Wildfires, which are becoming more frequent and severe due to climate change, also contribute to air pollution, releasing harmful particulates that can lead to respiratory and cardiovascular problems.

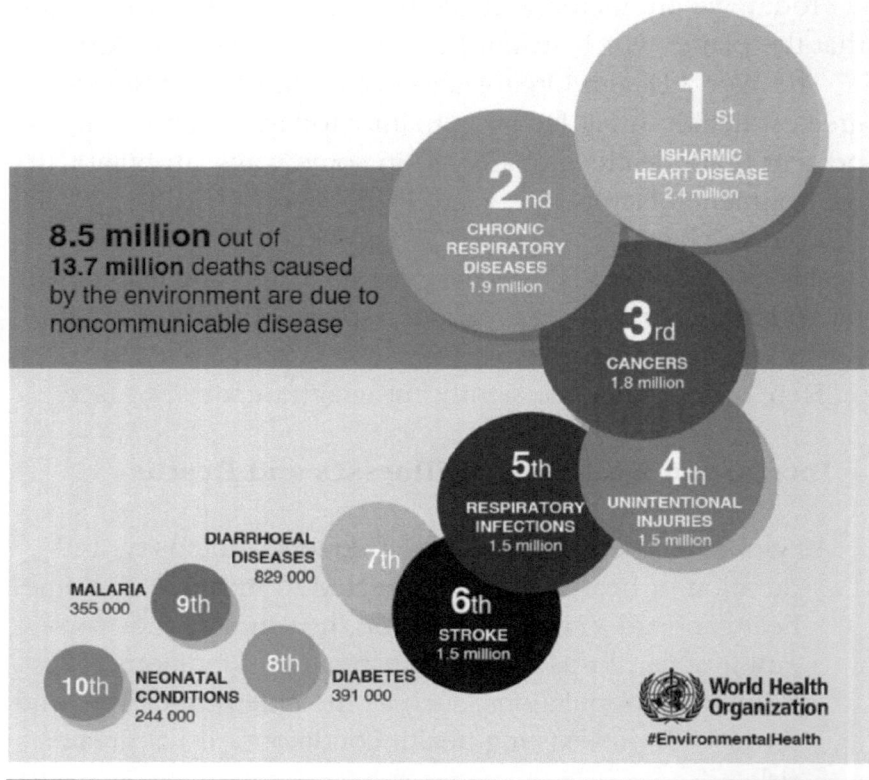

Figure 19.1   Top Ten Causes of Death from the Environment.

Spread of Infectious Diseases

Climate change is altering the habitats and life cycles of
insects such as mosquitoes and ticks. This can lead to the
spread of diseases like malaria, dengue fever, Zika virus,
and Lyme disease to new regions, including areas that
were previously too cold for these bugs to survive.

Waterborne Diseases

Warmer temperatures and changing precipitation patterns
affect water quality, leading to an increase in waterborne
diseases such as cholera and other diarrheal illnesses.

Flooding can contaminate drinking water supplies with pathogens, leading to outbreaks.

Impact on Food Security and Nutrition

Changes in climate, including increased temperatures, droughts, and extreme weather events, can negatively impact crop yields and food production. This can lead to food shortages, increased food prices, and malnutrition, particularly in vulnerable populations.

Climate change also impacts the nutritional value of what we grow. Rising levels of carbon dioxide can reduce the nutritional quality of crops, decreasing the protein, zinc, and iron content in staple foods, which can increase nutritional deficiencies.

Effects of Extreme Weather Events

The increased frequency and severity of extreme weather events such as hurricanes, floods, and storms can cause immediate injury and death. These events can also disrupt health care services, cause displacement, and lead to long-term health problems.

The Los Angeles wildfires that occurred in January of 2025 are a tragic cautionary tale of the impact of the environment on the health and wellbeing of humans.

Climate Change Is a Health Threat Multiplier

Climate change does not care about borders or bank accounts. Our most vulnerable populations bear its heaviest burden. The elderly, the economically disadvantaged, and those with pre-existing health conditions are most impacted by this environmental assault.[5]

Climate change is what public health experts and economists call a threat multiplier. It's a pervasive threat that stands to undermine and reverse decades of health progress.

The Epidemiology of Climate Change

Climate change refers to long-term shifts in temperatures and weather patterns.[6] And while some of these shifts are natural, the preponderance of data and scientific evidence points to human activities being the primary driver of climate change.

The primary cause is the release of greenhouse gases into the atmosphere.[7] These activities include burning fossil fuels like coal, oil, and gas, which generate greenhouse gas emissions that trap heat from the sun's rays inside the atmosphere, causing Earth's average temperature to rise. We call this global warming.[8]

The primary greenhouse gases causing climate change include carbon dioxide, methane, and nitrous oxide. These gases slow outgoing heat in the atmosphere and cause the planet to warm.[9]

Increases in greenhouse gases over the past several decades have been significant and are accelerating (Figure 19.2).

The combined warming influence of all long-lived greenhouse gases is measured and tracked by something known as the Annual Greenhouse Gas Index (AGGI).[10] Here's what this and other measures tell us about the rapid changes that are occurring:

- It took more than 200 years for the AGGI to go from 0 to 1 (to reach 100%), but only another 30 years for it to hit nearly 1.5 (an additional 50%).[11]
- By the end of 2021, the direct warming influence of human-produced greenhouse gases had risen 49% compared to 1990.

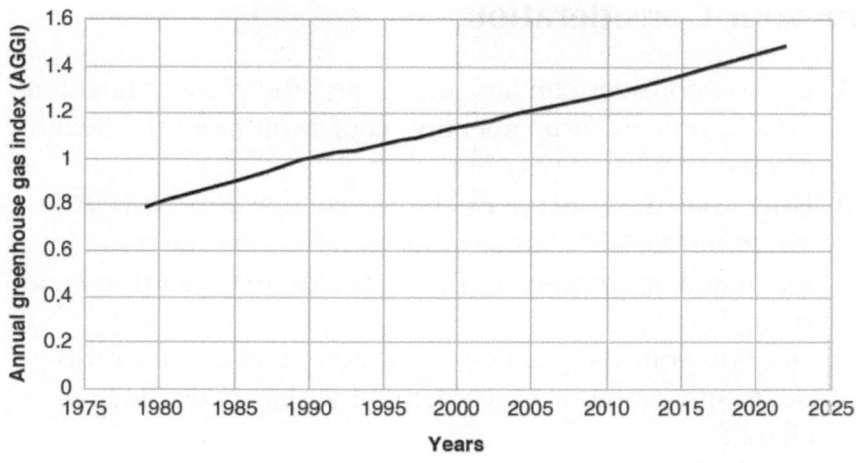

The AGGI–short for Annual Greenhouse Gas Index–reports the combined warming influence of all long-lived greenhouse gases as a fraction of their influence in 1990. NOAA Climate.gov graph, based on data from NOAA Global Monitoring Lab.

Figure 19.2   Annual Greenhouse Gas Index.

■ Most of the total heating imbalance (66%) is due to carbon dioxide. The annual rate of increase in atmospheric carbon dioxide over the past 60 years has been 100 times faster than previous natural increases.[12]

These statistics highlight the urgent need for global action to reduce greenhouse gas emissions.

The link between climate change and human health is undeniable and urgent. The health impacts of climate change are already being felt, and without immediate action, they will only worsen.

Protecting human health from the ravages of climate change requires a concerted effort at all levels—individual, community, national, and global. As we move forward, let us remember that the health of our planet and the health of its inhabitants are inextricably linked. Saving one means saving the other.

For Your Consideration:

1. Do you consider climate change and the planet's health to be a significant issue affecting your health and the health of others? Why or why not?
2. How does the concept of climate change as a *"health threat multiplier"* change your views on the need for integrated approaches to public health and environmental policy?
3. How do your daily actions and lifestyle choices contribute to mitigating or exacerbating the effects of climate change?
4. Do you believe climate change has significant implications for global health? If yes, what can you do to help foster greater awareness and action on climate change within your circle of influence?

Notes:

_____

_____

_____

_____

_____

_____

_____

_____

_____

_____

_____

_____

_____

_____

Endnotes

1. Institute of Medicine (US) Committee on Assuring the Health of the Public in the 21st Century. The Future of the Public's Health in the 21st Century. Washington (DC): National Academies Press (US); 2002. 2, Understanding Population Health and Its Determinants. Available from: https://www.ncbi.nlm.nih.gov/books/NBK221225/

2. Climate Change and Health, World Health Organization, October 12,2023, https://www.who.int/news-room/fact-sheets/detail/climate-change-and-health

3. Estimating Environmental Health Impacts, World Health Organization, https://www.who.int/activities/environmental-health-impacts

4. Summer 2024 Hottest Ever Recorded, EU Climate Change Monitor Says, 24 France, June 9, 2024, https://www.france24.com/en/europe/20240906-summer-2024-hottest-ever-recorded-on-the-planet-eu-climate-change-monitor-says

5. NASA. NASA Analysis Confirms 2023 as Warmest Year on Record, January 12, 2024, https://www.nasa.gov/news-release/nasa-analysis-confirms-2023-as-warmest-year-on-record/ational Institute of Environmental Health Sciences: Human Health Impacts of Climate Change (nih.gov)

6. What Is Climate Change?, United Nations, https://www.un.org/en/climatechange/what-is-climate-change

7. The Causes of Climate Change, NASA, https://science.nasa.gov/climate-change/causes/

8. Causes of Climate Change, United States Environmental Protection Agency, https://www.epa.gov/climatechange-science/causes-climate-change

9. The Causes of Climate Change, 174, https://science.nasa.gov/climate-change/causes/

10. Climate Change: Annual Greenhouse Gas Index, NOAA, June 17, 2022, https://www.climate.gov/news-features/understanding-climate/climate-change-annual-greenhouse-gas-index

11. Climate Change: Annual Greenhouse Gas Index, NOAA, June 17, 2022, https://www.climate.gov/news-features/understanding-climate/climate-change-annual-greenhouse-gas-index

12. Climate Change: Atmospheric Carbon Dioxide, NOAA, April 9, 2024, https://www.climate.gov/news-features/understanding-climate/climate-change-atmospheric-carbon-dioxide

Chapter 20

Sustainable Health Care

"The Earth does not belong to us. We belong to the Earth."

—*Chief Seattle*

As you wrap your mind around the implications of climate change and health, consider this: If the health care sector were a country, it would be the fifth largest emitter of greenhouse gases (GHG) on the planet.[1]

When it comes to climate change, health care is a significant contributor to the problem. Its total carbon footprint is equivalent to 4.4% of global greenhouse gas emissions.[2]

This relationship between health care and the environment is a glaring contradiction: As health care delivers care in the current model its environmental footprint harms the health of those they serve. This creates a vicious cycle of more people turning to the system for help which further exacerbates the problem.

The U.S. health care system is the top emitter of green-house gases (GHG) in health care worldwide. We're followed by China, and collectively the countries of the European

DOI: 10.4324/9781003600695-23

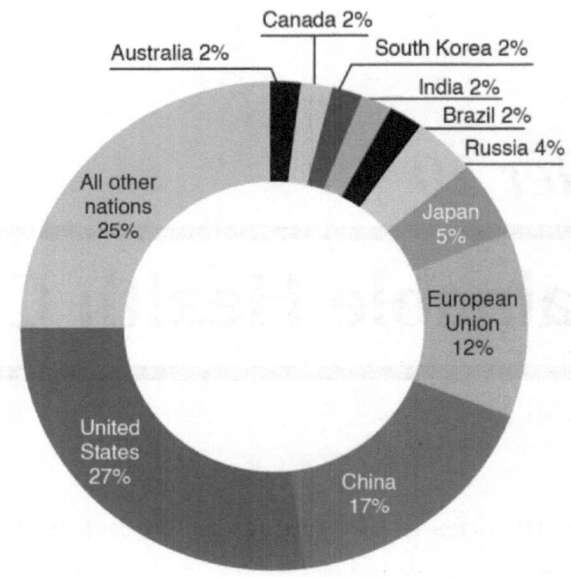

Figure 20.1 Top Ten Emitters as a Percentage of Global Health Care Footprint.

Source: Healthcare's Climate Footprint, Healthcare Without Harm, 2019.

Union. Together, this trio comprises more than half the world's total health care climate footprint (56%) (Figures 20.1).[3]

Within the US, the health care sector is responsible for 8.5% of GHG emissions.[4]

And so, it is only logical that the health system must do better to support the health of people and the planet going forward.[5]

Sustainable health care requires new approaches to health and medical care that ensure the health needs of the current population are met without compromising environmental, economic, or social resources for future generations.

So, what does a sustainable health system look like? The World Health Organization describes it as:

> An environmentally sustainable health system is one that improves, maintains or restores health, while

minimizing negative impacts on the environment and leveraging opportunities to restore and improve it, to the benefit of the health and well-being of current and future generations.[6]

Climate Change Is Important to Health Care Workers

Clinicians overwhelmingly want their employers to address climate change. Most clinical leaders and practicing physicians in U.S. health systems agree that it's important for the organization they work at to address climate change or minimize its impact on the environment.

At an individual level, three in four clinicians believe it's important to personally play a role in making this better when they are at work (Figure 20.2).[7]

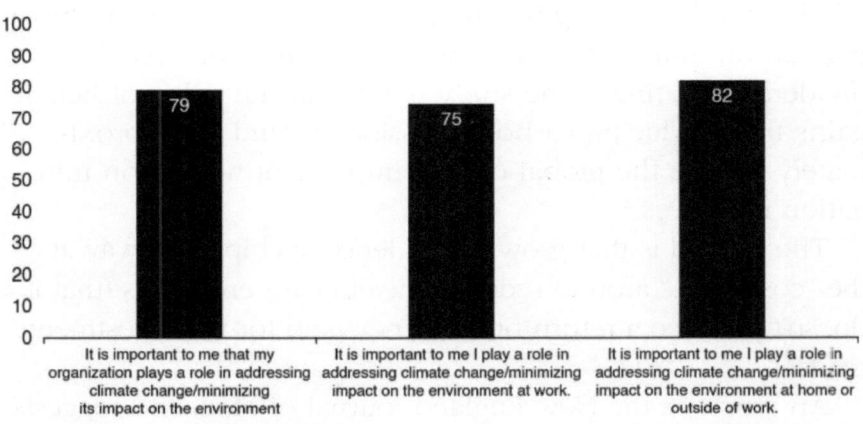

Figure 20.2   Majority of Clinicians Believe It's Important That the Health System They Work for Plays a Role in Addressing Climate Change.

Source: Arnav Shah and Lovisa Gustafsson, U.S. Health Care Workers Want Their Employers to Address Climate Change (Commonwealth Fund, Jan.2024). https://doi.org/10.26099/j1ra-t957

Given its contribution to greenhouse gas emissions, health care must act now to begin to reduce its own climate footprint.

Health policies and investments must be retooled to support decarbonization. If the health care sector — individual health care facilities, health systems, ministries of health, international and bilateral development agencies, and private health care organizations — all take action toward this goal, it can be achieved.

Effective sustainability and decarbonization efforts in health care require organization wide buy-in to new innovations, policies, and procedures. Such changes should be targeted at reducing waste and water consumption, adopting green building features, converting to renewable energy, and other activities to advance a more sustainable health system (Figure 20.3).

So how can we go about decarbonizing health care without drastically increasing costs?

There are two ways to look at the cost issue.

The first is to recognize that doing a better job or reducing carbon emissions will produce a measurable health dividend over time. One study notes that the value of health gains from reducing carbon emissions would be approximately double the global cost of implementing carbon mitigation measures.[8]

The second is that growing evidence is chipping away at the "cost myth" around reducing health care emissions (that it doesn't produce a return or efficiency gain for the investments made).

An article in the New England Journal of Medicine suggests that initiatives undertaken by health care organizations to reduce their carbon footprints could ultimately yield a positive return on investment while reducing greenhouse gases.[9]

Figure 20.3   Possible Elements of a National Sustainability Policy for Health Systems.

Source: World Health Organization, Environmentally sustainable health systems: a strategic document.

In her book *Greening Health Care: How Hospitals Can Heal the Planet*, former Environmental Stewardship Officer at Kaiser Permanente Kathy Gerwig provides examples such as installing on-site solar power, long-term purchases of new renewable energy generation, and waste reduction initiatives that can yield positive returns on investment while also reducing GHG emissions.[10]

The U.S. federal government has also stepped in with incentives for health care organizations to do better. With the Inflation Reduction Act of 2022, nonprofit organizations can now use the new tax credit provisions for renewable energy to support desired investments in buildings, energy infrastructure, and transportation, among others.

Investing in Green Energy and Sustainable Returns

The good news is that many health care organizations are waking up to the double-edged impact they can make on both health and the environment. They are making strides to become more environmentally responsible and sustainable.

Boston Medical Center (BMC) is part of a growing movement demonstrating that change is possible. It is a safety-net, academic medical center serving a large indigent patient population. BMC has committed to a strategic goal of reducing the environmental impact of its operations, both to improve the health of its community and to strengthen the resiliency of its critical care hospital infrastructure.

Beginning in 2011, BMC stepped up to its commitment to change. They redesigned their clinical campus, looked for product substitutions in the operating room and made greater use of solar power. The rooftop farm that sits atop BMCs power plant yields 5,000 pounds of produce annually. The bulk of the produce goes to the Preventive Food Pantry to help fight food insecurity among the people they serve.

Not only is BMC better serving its community in the present, it has reduced its carbon emissions from energy consumption by more than 90% which generates health benefits to future generations. [11]

Surgeons Go Green

Every year more than 300 million major operations take place in hospitals around the world. Some of the gases used in surgery are a thousand times more potent than our best-known greenhouse gas, carbon dioxide.

Most of these gases are expelled from patients' lungs and flushed outside into the atmosphere where they act to trap heat.

Work is underway at the University of Melbourne to leverage new technology to capture, store and potentially recycle surgical gases. The inspiration for this research effort comes from the construction of molecular models that allow scientists to design and generate materials known as co-ordination polymers, which contain holes large enough to hold small molecules.

The team is working to develop a family of "tuneable" polymers that can be tailored to fit individual anesthetic gases. Big holes for big molecules, snugger holes for smaller ones. If successful, this effort could provide the dual benefit of reducing global warming while reducing surgical costs.[12]

Decarbonizing Radiology

Philips, a global leader in health technology and Vanderbilt University Medical Center have been collaborating on research to decarbonize radiology.

The initial results of this work show that sustainable radiology initiatives can be both environmentally friendly and cost-effective. As new imaging machines replace older devices these can reduce carbon emissions by 17% and the total cost of ownership of imaging systems by up to 23%.[13]

The message of this chapter is simple: We cannot lead healthy lives if we live in an ailing world. Health care can and must do better.

The phrase *"do no harm"* is a mantra and an oath taken by medical students, doctors, nurses and all of those pledging to care for others in their health journey. Let us go forward with the expectation that health care organizations will apply *"do no harm"* to their efforts to protect and restore the planet that humans and other living creatures call home.

For Your Consideration:

1. How does the information about health care's large carbon footprint change your perspective on the relationship between health and environmental practices?
2. Should health care's mission of *"do no harm"* extend to the industry's impact on the environment?
3. How do you reconcile the need for high-quality health care with the imperative to reduce its environmental

impact? What compromises, if any, would be acceptable?

Notes:

_____
_____
_____
_____
_____
_____
_____
_____
_____
_____
_____
_____
_____
_____
_____
_____
_____
_____
_____
_____
_____
_____
_____
_____

_____
_____
_____
_____
_____
_____
_____
_____
_____
_____
_____
_____
_____
_____
_____
_____
_____
_____
_____
_____
_____
_____
_____
_____
_____
_____

Endnotes

1. Climate Crisis: Healthcare Is a Major Contributor, Global Report Finds. *The BMJ*, September 13, 2019, https://www.bmj.com/content/366/bmj.l5560

2. Climate Crisis: Healthcare Is a Major Contributor, Global Report Finds. *The BMJ,* September 13, 2019, https://www.bmj.com/content/366/bmj.l5560

3. Health Care's Climate Footprint How the Health Sector Contributes to the Global Climate Crisis and Opportunities for Action. Health Care Without Harm Climate-smart health care series Green Paper Number One, Produced in collaboration with Arup, September 2019. https://www.arup.com/insights/health cares-climate-footprint/

4. U.S. Health Care Workers Want Their Employers to Address Climate Change, The Commonwealth Fund, January 24, 2024, https://www.commonwealthfund.org/publications/issue-briefs/2024/jan/us-health-care-workers-want-employers-address-climate-change

5. Environmentally Sustainable Health Systems: A Strategic Document, World Health Organization, 2021, https://iris.who.int/handle/10665/340375?show=full

6. Environmentally Sustainable Health Systems: A Strategic Document, World Health Organization, 2021, https://iris.who.int/handle/10665/340375?show=full

7. U.S. Health Workers Want Employers to Address Climate Change, 183

8. Fast Facts on Climate Change, World Health Organization, https://cdn.who.int/media/docs/default-source/climate-change/fast-facts-on-climate-and-health.pdf?sfvrsn=157ecd81_5&download=true

9. Vivian S. Lee, Decarbonizing Health Care: Engaging Leaders in Change. *NEJM Catalyst,* April 19, 2023, https://catalyst.nejm.org/doi/full/10.1056/CAT.22.0433

10. Kathy Gerwig, *Greening Health Care: How Hospitals Can Heal the Planet,* 2014. Oxford Press, https://doi.org/10.1093/med/9780199385836.001.0001

11. Vivian S. Lee, Decarbonizing Health Care: Engaging Leaders in Change. *NEJM Catalyst,* 2023, 188, https://catalyst.nejm.org/doi/full/10.1056/CAT.22.0433.

12. Tunable Porous Coordination Polymers for the Capture, Recovery and Storage of Inhalation Anesthetics, Chemistry Europe, 2017, https://chemistry-europe.onlinelibrary.wiley.com/doi/full/10.1002/chem.201700389

13. Research from Philips and Vanderbilt Shows How Decarbonizing Healthcare Also Helps to Reduce Cost, Philips, November 29, 2023, https://www.usa.philips.com/a-w/about/news/archive/standard/news/press/2023/20231129-research-from-philips-and-vanderbilt-shows-how-decarbonizing-healthcare-also-helps-to-reduce-cost.html

Chapter 21

Welcome to the Intelligent Health Revolution

rev·o·lu·tion | \ re-və-'lü-shən

A: *a change of paradigm*

B: *a sudden, radical, or complete change*

The revolution has begun. Artificial Intelligence (AI) is pervasive in our daily lives and is now disrupting the world of health and medicine in ways not thought possible even a few years ago. In a world of *"intelligent everything"* there will be no room for unintelligent health.

What if we could detect heart disease in a single heartbeat or breast cancer before symptoms appear? How about unlimited, AI-assisted virtual health consults for one dollar a visit? Sound like more AI hype? It's not. Transformative health services are happening now.[1,2,3] They're driven by restless individuals and organizations unwilling to accept the status quo in health.

DOI: 10.4324/9781003600695-24

Such change could not come at a better time. Clinical and health leaders today are faced with an unrelenting set of challenges. Ever-expanding medical capabilities. Constrained resources and staff shortages. An increasingly diverse mix of patients and consumers whose needs only grow. The health status of individuals and populations is going in the wrong direction. Merely getting better with the tools we have will not deliver the results we need.

Forget about the stereotype of AI creating an impersonal, robot-controlled future. AI is set to deliver a different model that will eclipse current systems in delivering on the promises we make every day: To improve health while delivering greater value. To provide highly personalized experiences to health consumers. To restore clinicians to be the caregivers they want to be rather than the data entry clerks we're turning them into by forcing them to use systems and processes conceived decades ago.

The first shots in the Intelligence Revolution were fired years ago. You benefit from them whenever you go online,

Figure 21.1   Areas of Impact for AI.

Source: McKinsey & Company, Transforming health care with AI: The impact on the workforce and organizations.

use a smart app, or get directions. The pandemic showed us that humans are better and faster in solving big problems in health and medicine because of them.

Today every health care organization is making use of AI. In the future we will see two business models emerge that will be driven by how AI is applied.

Traditional Health Systems will leverage the power of AI to improve efficiencies in how care is provided.

We are also seeing the emergence of Intelligent Health Systems. These can be newly formed digital-first companies or the reinvention of Traditional Health Systems. The leadership of these organizations will focus on using AI to drive *new approaches* to overcome the age-old challenges of improving access, quality, effectiveness, and costs of health services.

Traditional Health Systems will use AI to make the currently delivery model more effective. Intelligent Health Systems will use AI as a vehicle to reimagine and improve consumer, patient and clinician experiences. They will do this across all touchpoints, experiences, and service delivery channels.

AI Augments and Enhances the Skills of Humans

As AI technology matures, it is poised to revolutionize health care, bringing about significant improvements in diagnosis, treatment, patient care, and operational efficiency.

Enhancing Diagnostic Accuracy and Speed

One of the most profound impacts of AI in health care is its ability to enhance diagnostic accuracy and speed. Traditionally, diagnosis relies heavily on the expertise and experience of medical professionals, which can vary widely. AI, however, can analyze vast amounts of medical data, including imaging, genetic information, and patient history, to identify patterns and anomalies that might elude even the most seasoned clinicians.

For instance, AI-powered imaging tools are already being used to detect early signs of conditions like cancer, cardiovascular diseases, and neurological disorders with remarkable precision. These tools can analyze radiology images much faster than humans and with fewer errors, leading to earlier detection and, consequently, more effective treatment. The application of AI in genomics is another area where it can predict the likelihood of hereditary diseases, allowing for preventive measures before the onset of symptoms.

Personalized Treatment Plans

AI's capability to analyze and learn from large datasets enables the creation of highly personalized treatment plans. Each patient is unique, and a one-size-fits-all approach is often insufficient. AI can consider individual differences in genetics, environment, lifestyle, and even microbiome composition to tailor treatments that are most likely to be effective for each person.

This approach is particularly beneficial in the field of oncology, where treatments can be highly variable. AI can help in designing personalized cancer therapies by analyzing the genetic makeup of both the patient and the tumor, leading to more targeted and effective interventions with fewer side effects. Similarly, in chronic disease management, AI can provide real-time recommendations based on continuous monitoring, thereby improving patient outcomes, and quality of life.

Improving Patient Care and Experience

AI also holds the promise of significantly improving patient care and experience. Virtual health assistants, powered by AI, can provide consumers and patients with 24/7 access to medical information, answer their queries, and even assist in managing chronic conditions by reminding them to take medications or schedule follow-up appointments. These AI-driven assistants can alleviate the burden on health care professionals, allowing them to focus on more complex cases.

Moreover, AI can enhance patient experience by enabling remote monitoring and telehealth services. With AI-driven wearable devices, patients and consumers can be monitored continuously for vital signs, and any deviations from the norm can trigger alerts to health care providers. This not only reduces the need for frequent hospital visits but also allows for timely intervention in case of emergencies, improving outcomes and reducing health care costs.

Streamlining Operations and Reducing Costs

Beyond direct patient care, AI can streamline health care operations, leading to significant cost reductions. Health care facilities often grapple with administrative inefficiencies, from scheduling and billing to inventory management. AI can automate many of these tasks, reducing errors and freeing up staff to focus on more critical functions.

For example, AI-driven predictive analytics can optimize hospital staffing by forecasting patient admissions and the required workforce. This ensures that hospitals are neither understaffed nor overstaffed, improving operational efficiency and reducing costs. Additionally, AI can help manage health care supply chains more effectively, ensuring that essential medications and equipment are available when needed, thereby minimizing waste and shortages.

Accelerating Drug Discovery and Development

The process of drug discovery and development is notoriously time-consuming and expensive. AI can accelerate this process by analyzing vast amounts of biological data to identify potential drug candidates more quickly and accurately than traditional methods. AI can also predict how these candidates will interact with the human body, reducing the likelihood of costly failures in later stages of development.

This capability was vividly demonstrated during the COVID-19 pandemic, where AI played a crucial role in identifying potential treatments and vaccines at an unprecedented speed. As AI continues to evolve, it will likely lead to the developing more effective drugs in shorter timeframes, addressing a wide range of diseases and conditions.

Ethical Considerations and Challenges

While the potential benefits of AI in health care are immense, it is important to acknowledge the ethical considerations and challenges that come with it. Issues such as data privacy, algorithmic bias, and the need for transparency in AI decision-making processes must be addressed to ensure that AI is used responsibly and equitably in health care.

AI Requires an Openness to Change

An important nuance with AI across all delivery models is that AI *enables humans* to change how they live and work. It's up to humans to adopt AI technologies. In doing so, athey must be willing to adapt to the changes brought about by AI. This important principle applies both to the organizations providing health services and those receiving such services.

Early adopters are already seeing real-world benefits and competitive advantages. And the *velocity of value* will only grow as AI solutions mature. These trends are beginning to permeate health care. They're creating almost unlimited opportunities to innovate health and medicine – For those who choose to use them wisely.

Another critical factor driving AI and intelligent health forward is what's happening in the rest of the world. The rise of intelligent consumers and their expectations is a reality. The question is not whether intelligent systems are becoming the norm, but rather how the health industry will adapt and keep up with the revolution that is already occurring.

Consumers and businesses expect smart systems to make their lives better. According to data from Accenture consumers and patients are already six times more likely to view AI as positively impacting health service delivery. This makes AI a competitive differentiator when it comes to acquiring patients and building consumer loyalty.[4]

Driven by AI the intelligent health revolution promises a healthier America. As we embrace these advancements, collaboration between AI, health care professionals, consumers, and policymakers will be pivotal. By harnessing AI's potential responsibly, we can create a future where health is personalized, accessible, and optimized for all.

In making this statement it's important to recognize that AI is not the answer to fixing health care. Humans are. We were smart enough to create artificial intelligence, but now we must harness it for the good it can do in health and medicine.

AI will not replace human expertise but will augment it, leading to a health care landscape that prioritizes prevention, early intervention, and individual well-being. Let us embrace this revolution and build a healthier, AI-enhanced health care system.

For Your Consideration:

1. How do you perceive the potential of AI to change the health care landscape, especially in terms of accessibility and quality of care?
2. Consider the ethical implications of AI in health care. What concerns might arise from an increased reliance on AI for diagnoses and treatment decisions? How should these be addressed?
3. Reflect on the balance between technology and human touch in health care. How can we ensure that AI enhances rather than replaces the essential human elements of caregiving?
4. As AI plays a larger role in health care, what changes do you think are necessary in medical education and training to prepare future health care professionals for this new era?

Notes:

_____

_____

_____

_____

_____

_____

_____

_____

_____

_____

_____

_____

_____

_____

_____

Endnotes

1. Mihaela Porumb, Ernesto Iadanza, Sebastiano Massaro, and Leandro Pecchia, A Convolutional Neural Network Approach to Detect Congestive Heart Failure. *Biomedical Signal Processing and Control Journal,* 55, January 2020, 101597.
2. Anne D'innocenzio and Tom Murphy, and Walmart's Sam's Club Launches Health Care Pilot to Members. *AP Business Writers,* 2019, https://www.usnews.com/news/us/articles/ 2019-09-26/walmarts-sams-club-launches-health-care-pilot-to-members
3. https://www.msn.com/en-us/health/other/amazing-ways-ai-tech-benefits-practitioners-and-patients-in-the-health care-industry-report/ar-BB1hIS3r
4. Weber Shandwick, AI-Ready or Not: Artificial Intelligence Here We Come!, https://www.webershandwick.com/news/article/ ai-ready-or-not-artificial-intelligence-here-we-come

Chapter 22

Welcome to the Planet of the Apps

"We take better care of our smartphones than ourselves. We know when the battery is depleted and recharge it."

—*Arianna Huffington*

Did you know that the average smartphone today has a million times more processing power than the NASA computers that sent humans to the moon?[1]

In a world where smartphones are seemingly becoming more intelligent than their users, health apps are emerging as the unsung heroes of our health and well-being. Clinically speaking, it's an emerging market, but these pocket-sized super-computers and other devices promise to transform our lives, one-step count at a time.

Our love affair with digital devices is strong and growing. One study indicates that the average number of interactions we have with digital devices is approaching 5,000 per day.

DOI: 10.4324/9781003600695-25

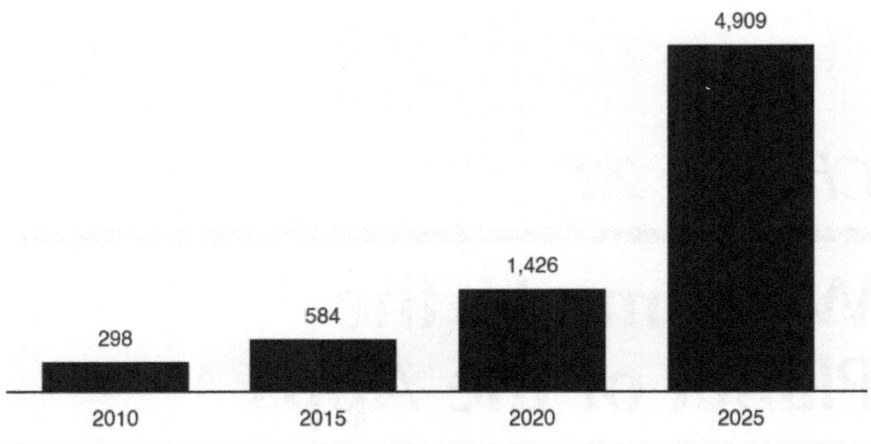

Figure 22.1   Digital Device Interactions Per Capita Per Day.

*Source: RBC Capital Markets: The Data Explosion Episode. www.rbccm.com/
en/gib/healthcare/episode/the_healthcare_data_explosion*

Much of this growth comes from consumers interested in
their health.

Today, about two-thirds of U.S. adults have used an app for
health-related purposes.[2]

In some ways, we can thank the pandemic for today's
mobile health movement. Before COVID, consumer health
apps were mainly interesting gadgets used by the *"quantified
self"* crowd. When the pandemic hit, health consumers used
their at-home time to download and use health apps to bridge
the care gap caused when COVID disrupted the traditional
delivery of health and medical services. In 2020 alone, the use
of health apps grew worldwide by 65%.[3]

Health apps, or more officially Mobile Health or mHealth
apps, are software programs on mobile devices that process
health-related data on or for their users. They are seamlessly
integrated into smartwatches, fitness bands, and even sensing
fabrics which are used in smart clothing and mattresses.

Health apps are increasingly being used by health-
conscious people and clinicians to maintain, improve, or manage the health of an individual or a population of people.

As an umbrella term, health apps include medical apps. Medical apps share the same technological functions and devices with health professionals, patients, and family caregivers being the main user groups. Medical apps are intended for clinical and medical purposes and may be legally regulated as mobile medical devices.[4]

Collectively, health apps incorporate services such as health and wellness, remote patient monitoring, and health information and education that typically fall into three categories[5]:

Health Monitoring, Early Detection and Prevention

Consumer health apps act as vigilant companions, monitoring vital signs and symptoms. They alert users to irregularities, prompting timely action. For instance, heart rate variability apps can signal stress, while sleep trackers identify sleep disorders. Early detection translates to better outcomes and reduced health care costs.

Chronic Disease Management

For individuals with chronic conditions, consumer health apps are lifelines. Diabetes management apps track blood glucose levels, medication adherence, and diet. Asthma apps monitor inhaler usage and trigger avoidance. As chronic diseases become more prevalent, these apps will play an essential role in improving quality of life.

Mental Health and Well-Being

Stress, anxiety, and depression affect millions globally. Mental health apps offer coping strategies, meditation sessions, and mood tracking. They destigmatize seeking help and provide a lifeline during crises. The future holds AI-driven emotional intelligence apps that adapt to users' emotional states and offer personalized support.

Health apps are continuing to evolve to become powerful tools that bridge the gap between individuals and their well-being. These digital companions offer a myriad of benefits, from promoting healthy lifestyles to helping you and your care team in managing chronic conditions.

Here are some of the value factors health apps provide:

Information

Health apps use sensors, GPS, and internet connections to track vitals like heart rate and sleep time. Information that helps achieve fitness goals, such as the number of steps taken in a day, calories burned per exercise, and the number of strokes it took to reach the other side of a pool, can also be provided by apps.

Mobile apps present health information in the form of infographics and tables, which are easy for users to understand and can be customized based on the user's needs.

Education

Mobile apps improve users' health education by providing personalized feedback and coaching based on their health data and goals. Many health apps provide information on specific diseases and health conditions. Some provide clinically validated advice and guidance on how best to manage symptoms related to specific conditions.

Monitoring

Mobile apps are useful for individuals at risk of developing chronic diseases like diabetes, asthma, or heart disease because they allow them to regularly monitor things like blood glucose levels and peak flow measurements. It enables them to make changes in diet or exercise habits as needed before the onset of more serious symptoms such as high blood pressure or chest pain is left untreated too long.

Diagnosis

Mobile apps can assist in diagnosis by allowing users to input their symptoms and receive a potential diagnosis. Recent advancements in the use of things like generative AI are improving the ability of providers and consumers in making accurate diagnoses early. Apps are becoming increasingly accurate as technology progresses.[6]

Treatment

Patients are more likely to adhere to the prescribed treatment plan when they use mobile apps to track their medication usage. Offering reminders based on clinical guidelines or evidence-based studies on effective treatments for certain diseases is one way in which mobile apps can improve treatment adherence.

Support

When consumers need to contact their doctor or health professional, waiting on hold and navigating their office's automated phone system can be frustrating. With a mobile app, consumers receive notifications when the doctor has seen your message or video call invite, send secure messages and have video calls from their device; and schedule appointments or consultations in the app.

Making Health Care Seamless

Health apps provide quick and easy access, transfer, and tracking of health information, as well as interactive displays and interventions that allow users to be highly engaged in promoting health outcomes and changing health-related behaviors.[7] Thus, health-related apps have a great potential to aid a wide range of target audiences with a variety of health issues.[8]

For consumers, health apps put information and tools at their fingertips. Whether it's tracking daily steps, monitoring heart rate, or logging meals, health apps encourage active participation in one's health journey. By fostering self-awareness and accountability, they transform passive patients into informed advocates.

Consumer health apps seamlessly integrate with wearables to collect data that focuses on continuous monitoring of a consumer's daily activities. This real-time data collection enhances app accuracy and can serve as an early warning system to prevent or mitigate adverse health events from happening. The synergy between wearables and apps will redefine preventive health.

For health care providers, health apps add an important new dimension to monitoring and managing a variety of health and medical conditions. The value comes when data from health apps is coordinated and connected to the longitudinal record of consumers and patients.

The evolution of the health apps market is underway. Over time this will become a disruptive force to the existing system. The new capabilities of providing "care anywhere" will be used by innovative health organizations seeking to improve both the experience and the level of health of those they serve. Given the rapidity of technological advances and consumer expectations those health organizations that go slow may be left behind.

Challenges of an Evolving Market

The synergy between mobile devices and health apps is already redefining preventive health. As they become more pervasive here are some of the issues that must be resolved before consumers and clinicians can take full advantage of this movement.

1. **Quality and Accuracy:** Not all consumer health apps are created equal. While some apps considered "medical grade" are required to meet certain specific standards, other apps lack rigorous validation or provide inaccurate information.
2. **Data Security and Privacy Concerns:** The increasing adoption of digital platforms raises valid concerns about the security and privacy of health care data.
3. **Integration and Interoperability:** Similar to other systems used in health care, consumer health apps often operate in silos, making it challenging to integrate them seamlessly with existing health care systems.
4. **Regulatory Compliance:** Navigating the complex landscape of health care regulations and compliance standards is challenging. Providers and payers must ensure that consumer health apps adhere to HIPAA and other relevant guidelines[2].
5. **Provider-Patient Communication:** The use of health apps can alter the dynamics of provider-patient interactions. Ensuring effective communication and shared decision-making while incorporating app-generated data is crucial[2].
6. **Evidence-Based Practices:** While many health apps claim to improve health outcomes, not all have robust evidence supporting their efficacy. Providers and payers need to identify apps backed by scientific research and avoid promoting ineffective solutions[2].

Do Health Apps Improve Health?

Despite the evolution and increased use of health apps, their effectiveness is not yet fully understood as the field of research related to health apps is still in a nascent stage[9]

Current research shows that mobile health applications in general are having a positive impact on health-related behaviors and clinical health outcomes. Application users were more satisfied with using mobile health applications to manage their health in comparison to users of conventional care.[10]

There is also evidence that use of health apps does impact improvement in both short-term metrics (such as a reduction in patients' blood glucose and glycated hemoglobin levels) and longer-term metrics (such as a reduction in hospital visits and medical expenses).

On average, patients who adopted mHealth achieve higher levels of exercise, consume healthier food with lower calories, walked more steps, and slept longer on a daily basis.[11]

The Road Ahead

Digital health apps are already helping consumers and clinicians alike. They are empowering both through easier access to advice and support while improving their understanding and management of health conditions.

Going forward we will see a new set of digital diagnostic and treatment paradigms emerge including AI-driven diagnostics, personalized treatment plans, and predictive analytics. Imagine an app that predicts a migraine or asthma attack based on weather changes or recommends tailored exercise routines for genetic profiles. The journey has just begun.

Health apps will play an important role in delivering a new *"care anywhere"* health model. Consumers and patients will be more engaged in managing their health through digitally enabled care pathways. Broader access to health care services, including participation and awareness of a wider population will drive measurable improvements in health metrics.

Evidence-based health apps will be integrated into established clinical treatment pathways, with the aim of both improving outcomes of current treatments and increasing access to specialized, and, where relevant, personalized, therapies.

Health apps also have the potential to improve sustainability of health care. They will help reduce patient and clinician travel, allow for remote monitoring, treatment, and remote medication management.

Consumer health apps empower individuals, enhance preventive care, and revolutionize health care. As technology evolves, their value will continue to soar, making health a truly personal and proactive endeavor.

We are seeing the emergence of the *"Planet of the Apps."* An increasing number of health apps are delivering experiences that meet the expectations of today's consumers, including younger, "digital natives." Done right, these data-driven technologies will spur digitization and automation capabilities that improve health, lower costs and delight consumers.

As consumer expectations grow, innovative health organizations will take advantage of this trend to automate core processes, strengthen their partnership with health consumers and reposition themselves as leaders in the evolving health and well-being landscape.

For Your Consideration:

1. How do health apps reshape our relationship with our own health? Do you think they encourage healthier habits?
2. What are some of the key challenges and risks associated with health apps, such as data security, accuracy, and regulatory concerns? How should these be addressed?
3. Do you believe that the widespread use of health apps could genuinely reduce health care costs and improve overall health outcomes, or are there limitations to their effectiveness?
4. What is your current experience in the use of health apps?

Notes:

_____

_____

_____

_____

_____

_____

_____

_____

_____

_____

_____

_____

_____

_____

_____

_____

Endnotes

1. Smartphone Is Millions of Times Faster Than NASA's 1960s Computers. *ZME Science*, May 11, 2023, https://www.zmescience.com/feature-post/technology-articles/computer-science/smartphone-power-compared-to-apollo-432/
2. Nearly Two-Thirds of US Consumers Are Mobile Health App Users. *eMarketer*, February 21, 2023, https://www.insiderintelligence.com/content/nearly-two-thirds-of-us-consumers-mobile-health-app-users
3. COVID-19 Growth in Medical App Downloads by Country 2020, Statista, October 20, 2022, https://www.statista.com/statistics/1181413/medical-app-downloads-growth-during-covid-pandemic-by-country/
4. The Definitions of Health Apps and Medical Apps from the Perspective of Public Health and Law: Qualitative Analysis of an Interdisciplinary Literature Overview, JMIR Publications, October 31, 2022, https://mhealth.jmir.org/2022/10/e37980
5. mHealth – Statistics and Facts, Statistica, January 10, 2024 https://www.statista.com/topics/2263/mhealth/#topicOverview
6. Ruth Hailu, Andrew Beam, and Ateev Mehrotra, ChatGPT-Assisted Diagnosis: Is the Future Suddenly Here?, *STAT*, February 13, 2023, https://www.statnews.com/2023/02/13/chatgpt-assisted-diagnosis/
7. Edwin D. Boudreaux, Molly E. Waring, Rashelle B. Hayes, Rajani S. Sadasivam, Sean Mullen, and Sherry Pagoto, Evaluating and Selecting Mobile Health Apps: Strategies for Health Care Providers and Health Care Organizations. *Translational Behavioral Medicine*, 4(4), 2014, 363–371. [PMC free article] [PubMed] [Google Scholar]
8. Jing Zhao, Becky Freeman, and Mu Li, Can Mobile Phone Apps Influence People's Health Behavior Change? An Evidence Review. *Journal of Medical Internet Research*, 18(11), 2016, e287.
9. Free, Caroline, Gemma Phillips, Louise Watson, Leandro Galli, Lambert Felix, Phil Edwards, Vikram Patel, and Andy Haines, The Effectiveness of Mobile-Health Technologies to Improve Health Care Service Delivery Processes: A Systematic Review and Meta-Analysis. *PLoS Medicine*, 10(1), 2013, e1001363.

10. Myeunghee Han and Eunjoo Lee, Effectiveness of Mobile Health Application Use to Improve Health Behavior Changes: A Systematic Review of Randomized Controlled Trials. *Healthcare Informatics Research*, 24(3), July 2018, 207–226. http://dx.doi.org/10.4258/hir.2018.24.3.207. Epub 2018 July 31. PMID: 30109154; PMCID: PMC6085201.
11. Anindya Ghose, Do Health Apps Really Make Us Healthier? *Harvard Business Review*, May 7, 2021, https://hbr.org/2021/05/do-health-apps-really-make-us-healthier

Chapter 23

Intelligent Aging Is Health Care's Moonshot

"It's not how old you are, it's how you are old."

—Jules Renard

It was the summer of 1965 when Medicare was signed into law, guaranteeing that the federal government would manage the provision and cost of medical care for all seniors. In doing so, President Lyndon Johnson proudly declared, *"No longer will older Americans be denied the healing miracle of modern medicine. No longer will illness crush and destroy the savings that they have so carefully put away over a lifetime."*[1]

As the country's then 19 million seniors celebrated, little note was taken of the 76 million children who were part of a generation that would come to be known as the "baby boomers."[2,3]

A nation of people once very young is today growing older by the minute. Ten thousand boomers turn 70 every day. Medicare covers 62 million beneficiaries today. This will swell to over 80 million beneficiaries by 2030.[4,5] As this tectonic demographic shift happens, there is another essential fact to

 DOI: 10.4324/9781003600695-26

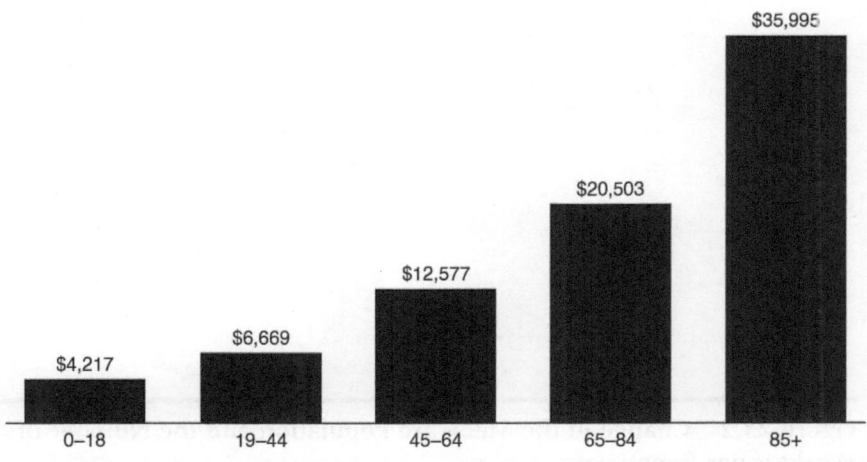

Figure 23.1   Medical Spending Increases Rapidly with Age.

Sources: Centers for Medicare and Medicaid Services, Peter G. Peterson Foundation.

consider: On average, those 65 and older consume five times more health resources than those under 65 (Figure 23.1).[6]

Medicare already accounts for 17% of all U.S. health expenditures, one-eighth of the federal budget, and 2 percent of gross domestic product.[7] There are many challenges to Medicare. One is the sheer cost and results of how it works. The other is the declining number of workers who are taxed to pay for it.

Caring for aging boomers and other Medicare recipients will stress the economic well-being of the working-age population. The number of taxpaying workers per Medicare beneficiary has declined from 4.6 during the program's early years to 2.9 today. By 2030, this number is projected to be 2.3 (Figure 23.2).[8]

The hypergrowth of Medicare beneficiaries multiplied by a 5X consumption factor is problematic. Add medical inflation, expected staffing shortfalls, and a decreasing number of workers to pay for it, and you grasp the magnitude of the problem.

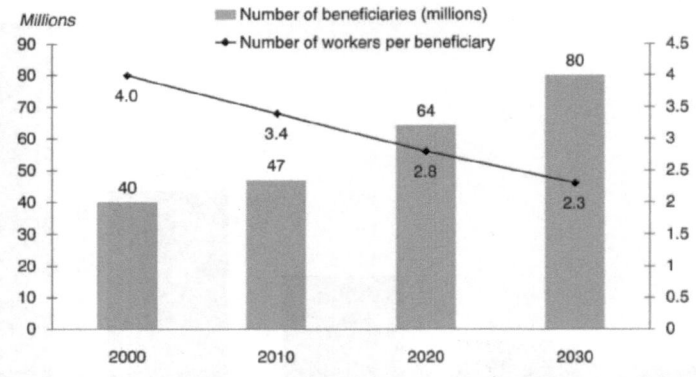

Figure 23.2   Change in the Medicare Population and the Number of Workers per Beneficiary.

Source: 2021 Medicare Trustee Report, www.cms.gov/Research-Statistics-Data-and-Systems/Statistics-Trends-and-Reports/ReportsTrustFunds

Changing Outcomes by Changing the Model

A paradigm shift is needed to better manage older citizens' needs and curb rising costs. There are many moves that can be made to move us in a better direction.

> **Reactive to proactive:** As noted throughout this book, the delivery and payment for health and medical services are based on a "break-fix" model. A greater focus on preventive services and value-based care models will proactively focus more on the overall holistic health of populations rather than episodic and transaction-based treatments. They will balance investments in "care anywhere" services with desired outcomes. One of the top beneficiaries of this model is the Boomer generation whose health care needs will only grow as they age.
> When it comes to the health and well-being of older people, much of what needs to be done comes down

to preventing and better managing chronic conditions. Those aged 65 and over need help with health conditions that can be better monitored and managed with preventative, lifestyle, and community-based services.

Beyond chronic conditions, helping older Americans be healthy, safe, and independent includes providing non-medical solutions that have a significant impact on health and well-being.

Matching Lifespan with Healthspan

There is growing evidence that a longevity revolution is underway. In his book, *The Science and Technology of Growing Young*, Sergey Young foresees a time when the average citizen can be expected to live well into their 100s. If you think this sounds far-fetched, consider the fact that lifespan has more than doubled in the last 100 years.[9]

As we extend the amount of time the average human lives, the real issue is not lifespan but healthspan. Lifespan is the total number of years we live. Healthspan is how many of those years we have an acceptable level of health and well-being.

Rather than worrying about dying too young, many people today worry about living too long without sufficient quality of life. In the US, the difference between life expectancy, or lifespan, and healthy life expectancy, or healthspan, is almost ten years.[10]

As the population of older Americans continues to grow, there is an increasing need for innovative approaches to health and wellness. Traditional health care systems have long emphasized reactive rather than proactive care, primarily treating illnesses after they occur.

New models of care focus instead on preventive measures, holistic well-being, and social support systems explicitly tailored to the aging population. From advancements in technology to community-driven wellness programs, these new approaches aim to keep older Americans healthy, engaged, and independent for as long as possible.

There are many opportunities today that have the potential to enhance the quality of life and reduce health care costs for older Americans.

Emphasis on Preventive Care and Early Detection

Preventive care has always been important, but it is particularly crucial for older adults who face a higher risk of chronic illnesses like heart disease, diabetes, and cancer. Today, some health care organizations are implementing proactive measures, such as annual wellness visits, health screenings, and personalized health plans.

For instance, the Medicare Annual Wellness Visit offers a valuable opportunity for seniors to consult with health care providers about lifestyle changes, vaccinations, and screenings that help identify potential health issues before they become more serious.[11] Early detection of diseases allows for more effective and less invasive treatments, which ultimately contributes to a higher quality of life and potentially lower medical costs.

Technological Innovations in Aging Care

With the rise of digital health technologies, aging care is more accessible than ever. Telemedicine, for example, allows seniors to receive health care consultations from the comfort of their homes, reducing the need for transportation and minimizing exposure to infectious diseases. Telemedicine also helps overcome barriers for those in rural or underserved areas who may struggle to access in-person health care.

Wearable devices and health-monitoring apps further enhance the capacity for independent living among older

adults. These devices can track vital signs, detect falls,
and remind users to take their medications, alerting
caregivers or health care providers if an anomaly is
detected. Companies like Fitbit, Apple, and Samsung
are integrating more health-tracking features into their
devices, making them an integral part of aging care.
Artificial intelligence (AI) is also revolutionizing aging care
by enabling predictive analytics and personalized health
care recommendations. AI-powered platforms can analyze
data from wearables, health records, and other sources
to predict health risks, allowing for timely intervention.
AI chatbots, for instance, can provide social engagement,
mental stimulation, and reminders, all of which are particularly beneficial for seniors living alone.

Social and Community Support Programs

Social isolation is one of the most significant challenges
older Americans face, as it can lead to depression, cognitive decline, and a weakened immune system.[12] To
address this, community-centered wellness programs and
senior centers are becoming central to healthy aging.
Programs like Village-to-Village Network, for example,
empower seniors to stay in their homes while accessing
resources and assistance in their neighborhoods.[13] This
model allows seniors to age in place, fostering a sense of
community and independence.
Intergenerational programs are another way to address
isolation by connecting older adults with younger generations. These initiatives can range from school mentorships
to tech tutoring sessions, providing both parties with
social and educational benefits. Engaging in these programs helps seniors remain mentally active and socially
connected, significantly contributing to their emotional
well-being.

Holistic and Integrative Health Approaches

Holistic health models are increasingly being recognized for their benefits in aging care. By addressing physical, emotional, and mental well-being as interconnected elements, holistic approaches go beyond treating symptoms and instead focus on overall wellness.

Integrative health programs may combine conventional medicine with complementary practices such as meditation, yoga, or acupuncture, helping to manage stress, reduce pain, and improve mobility and flexibility.

Nutrition-focused programs are also integral to this model. Malnutrition is a common issue among older adults, and poor nutrition can lead to increased susceptibility to illness and delayed recovery from medical procedures.[14] Nutrition counseling and meal programs, such as Meals on Wheels, not only provide nutritious meals but also offer regular wellness check-ins, which can help combat loneliness and malnutrition simultaneously.

Financial and Insurance Innovations to Support Aging Health Needs

One of the primary barriers to accessing quality health care is affordability. Medicare and Medicaid have made strides in covering preventive services, but many seniors face high out-of-pocket costs for ongoing care. Insurance companies and policymakers are exploring new models of insurance that can help ease these burdens. Medicare Advantage plans, for example, often cover additional benefits such as fitness programs, transportation to medical appointments, and in some cases, over-the-counter medications, and assistive devices.

In addition, "value-based care" is a growing trend in health care, focusing on rewarding providers based on patient outcomes rather than the number of services provided. By incentivizing providers to deliver high-quality, cost-effective care, this model aims to create a system that prioritizes patient well-being and reduces unnecessary hospitalizations and medical procedures.

Aging-in-Place and Home Modification Programs

Many seniors prefer to age in place, remaining in their homes rather than moving to assisted living facilities. To support this, aging-in-place programs focus on home modifications that enhance safety and accessibility. Simple changes, such as installing bathroom grab bars or widening doorways for wheelchair access, can significantly reduce the risk of falls and injuries. Nonprofit organizations like Rebuilding Together provide free or low-cost home modifications to seniors, allowing them to live independently and safely.

In addition to physical modifications, services like home health aides and meal delivery are becoming more accessible through insurance coverage and community programs. These services enable seniors to receive the care they need without leaving their homes, which is particularly valuable for those with limited mobility or chronic illnesses.

As the older adult population grows, innovative models for health and wellness are essential to ensure that Americans can age with dignity, independence, and optimal health. By combining preventive care, technology, community support, holistic approaches, financial innovations, and home-based care, these new models create a comprehensive framework for supporting older adults. In addition to enhancing the lives of seniors, these initiatives hold the promise of reducing health care costs and improving outcomes on a national scale.

For Your Consideration:

1. The chapter discusses the importance of closing the gap between lifespan (time you live) and healthspan (quality of time). How important is this issue and what actions might be taken to close this gap?
2. Do you think the societal view of aging will need to shift in order to better support the growing population of older citizens, especially in terms of health care services?
3. The chapter highlights the increasing gap between the number of workers who are taxed to financially support Medicare and Medicare beneficiaries. What changes in policy or health care models might be necessary to ensure the sustainability of Medicare in the future?

Notes:

Endnotes

1. Amy Finkelstein and Robin McKnight, What Did Medicare Do (And Was It Worth It)?, NBER Working Paper No. 11609, April 2006, http://www.nber.org/papers/w11609
2. Older Americans 2016: Key Indicators of Well-Being, http://www.seniorcare.com/featured/aging-america/
3. America's Children: Key National Indicators of Well-Being, 2021 U.S. Census Bureau, Current Population Reports. https://www.childstats.gov/AMERICASCHILDREN/tables/pop1.asp
4. The Next Generation of Medicare Beneficiaries, MedPac Report to the Congress: Medicare and the Health Care Delivery System. 2015, http://www.medpac.gov/docs/default-source/reports/chapter-2-the-next-generation-of-medicare-beneficiaries-june-2015-report-.pdf#:~:text=The%20number%20of%20taxpaying%20workers%20per%20Medicare%20beneficiary,projected%20by%20the%20Medicare%20Trustees%20to%20be%202.3.
5. 2021 Medicare Beneficiaries at a Glance, CMS. https://www.cms.gov/Research-Statistics-Data-and-Systems/Statistics-Trends-and-Reports/Beneficiary-Snapshot/Bene_Snapshot
6. James Lubitz, Linda G. Greenberg, Yelena Gorina, Lynne Wartzman, and David Gibson, Three Decades of Health Care Use by the Elderly, 1965–1998. *Health Aff (Millwood)*, 20, 2001, 19–32.
7. Medicare and Its Impact, National Bureau of Economic Research, April 1, 2006, http://www.nber.org/digest/apr06/w11609.html
8. Medicare 2021 Trustee Report, CMS, https://www.cms.gov/Research-Statistics-Data-and-Systems/Statistics-Trends-and-Reports/ReportsTrustFunds
9. Max Roser, Twice as Long – Life Expectancy Around the World, Our World in Data, October 8, 2018. https://ourworldindata.org/life-expectancy-globally
10. Ken Dychtwald, Lifespan versus Healthspan, September 2, 2021, LinkedIn. https://www.linkedin.com/pulse/lifespan-versus-healthspan-ken-dychtwald/
11. Your Annual Wellness Visit, Medicare.gov, https://www.medicare.gov/coverage/yearly-wellness-visits

12. Social Isolation, Loneliness in Older People Pose Health Risks, National Institute on Aging, April 23, 2019, https://www.nia.nih.gov/news/social-isolation-loneliness-older-people-pose-health-risks#:~:text=Research%20has%20linked%20social%20isolation%20and%20loneliness%20to,depression%2C%20cognitive%20decline%2C%20Alzheimer%E2%80%99s%20disease%2C%20and%20even%20death.
13. Village to Village Network, https://www.vtvnetwork.org/
14. Malnutrition in Seniors, National Council on Aging, https://www.ncoa.org/older-adults/health/diet-nutrition/malnutrition/

Chapter 24

Changing Our Health Investment Strategy

"The measure of intelligence is the ability to change."

—*Albert Einstein*

Changing health care requires a fundamental shift in how we approach investments in a system we are all dependent upon. Remember the idea from Chapter 17 about thinking differently. This is where it applies in full force.

Improving health care is, in many ways, a clear example of *"following the money."* How we allocate our health care dollars sets the course for a future that's more efficient, equitable, and effective.

As we've explored throughout this book, today's system operates on a break-fix model. It's a reactive setup where health care providers are paid per service, test, or procedure. This encourages addressing issues only once they emerge. More services mean more pay for hospitals and doctors, regardless of whether those services actually improve health outcomes.

DOI: 10.4324/9781003600695-27

There are few direct incentives to keep patients and consumers healthy in the first place.

The key to bending the cost curve of health care isn't identifying services that generate savings. Instead, it's about a broader shift—redirecting our focus and resources from low-value to high-value care. High-value care is about building a long-term foundation that offers all Americans a real opportunity to become healthier and happier than they are today.

By reallocating health care dollars, we can achieve better health outcomes without increasing spending. This means cutting back on costly, low-impact services while investing in those that deliver greater economic and health value. Put simply, we can save more lives—and improve quality of life—for the same financial outlay.

With that in mind, here are some of the most promising opportunities for rethinking our health care investment strategy.

Value-Based Care

Value-based care is a model that flips current economic incentives around. It ties the amount that health care providers earn for their services to the *results they deliver for their patients, such as the quality, equity, and cost of care.*

Through financial incentives and other methods, value-based care programs focus on holding hospitals, doctors and other health providers accountable for improving outcomes. It gives them greater flexibility to deliver the right care at the right time and incentivizes the value delivered rather than the volume of things done.[1]

Done right, value-based care helps health consumers maintain their health, and get better when they are sick while also keeping costs down.

Various approaches to value-based care are being tested in the public and private sectors today.

The Centers for Medicare and Medicaid Services (CMS) has taken a leading role in testing voluntary and mandatory programs with hospitals, physician groups, health plans, and other health care entities.

One example is the voluntary Medicare Shared Savings Program. This allows providers to form groups called accountable care organizations (ACOs). ACOs can earn financial rewards by taking responsibility for caring for a defined group of Medicare beneficiaries and improving the care they receive. This is done through better coordination of services.

CMS aims to have all Medicare beneficiaries, and most Medicaid beneficiaries enrolled in accountable care programs by 2030, and the agency is committed to improving health equity through its value-based initiatives.

And while participation in value-based care programs is on the rise, many health care providers are still not onboard. Health care organizations that are leaning into value-based care are seeing good results.

For example, Humana's value-based care platform reduced total health care costs by 15% compared with traditional fee-for-service Medicare costs. Humana also reported a 26% higher Health care Effectiveness Data and Information Set ("HEDIS") quality score in its value-based care program compared to its fee-for-service payment system.[2]

Proactive Public Health

Look closely at the history of health care and you'll see that most progress in measurably improving health and longevity hasn't come from breakthrough drugs or heroic interventions. Instead, it comes from what we commonly refer to as public health.

7%	**$88**	**$4.5B**
Decrease in mortality rates that would result from a 10% increase in public health spending	Benefits yielded from every $1 invested in public health	Funding that experts say is needed to ensure equitable and sustained foundational public health services for all

Figure 24.1   Public Health Spending by the Numbers.

Source: Top Ten Ways to Improve Health and Health Equity, Center for American Progress.

The U.S. public health system is comprised of various federal, state, and local agencies that are proactively dedicated to disease prevention and health promotion. These agencies often toil in the background to deliver a wide range of public health interventions that are largely responsible for the nation's increased life expectancy. This includes promoting clean air and water; improving sanitation and food safety; creating safer environments that lead to fewer injuries; services that focus on helping vulnerable populations and increasing the uptake of vaccinations that protect against infectious diseases.

Evidence shows that investments in public health initiatives not only produce health gains, but also translate into greater financial returns beyond what was originally invested (Figure 24.1).

For example, a study of public health expenditures in California demonstrated that a $10 increase in per capita spending led to a 0.6 percent increase in the proportion of the population in very good or excellent health and reduced all-cause mortality by 9.1 per 100,000.[3] The collective benefit of investments made in public health suggests that every dollar California invested in public health resulted in $67 to $88 of benefits to society.[4]

More granular findings show that investments in public health services are linked to improvements in specific health outcomes. A study of maternal and child health public health programs found that spending increases in these programs was associated with reductions in the incidence of low birth-weight rates in Florida and Washington counties. They also showed a reduction in health disparities.[5,6]

Other estimates show that for every $1 invested in public health interventions focused on reducing common chronic conditions such as diabetes and cardiovascular disease, at least $5 in health spending can be saved.[7]

Despite overwhelming evidence that each dollar invested in public health often returns more than one dollar in health and financial benefits, spending for public health is declining in America (Figure 24.2).

A Shift toward Population Health

Population health is a term that is widely used in health care circles but not universally understood.

The World Health Organization (WHO) defines population health as *"the health outcomes of a group of individuals, including the distribution of such outcomes within the group."*[8] As noted in Chapter 10, population health focuses on interrelated conditions and factors that influence the health of populations over a lifetime known as Social Determinants of Health (SDOH). These include the conditions in which people are born, grow, live, work, and age, along with the wider set of forces and systems shaping the conditions of daily life.

Population health involves understanding and addressing the diverse factors that influence health outcomes across different populations.

A group can be a geographic region, such as a country or community, but can also be other groups, such as employees, ethnic groups or disabled persons.

Population health evaluates and attempts to influence the conditions and factors that impact the health of populations over lifetimes.

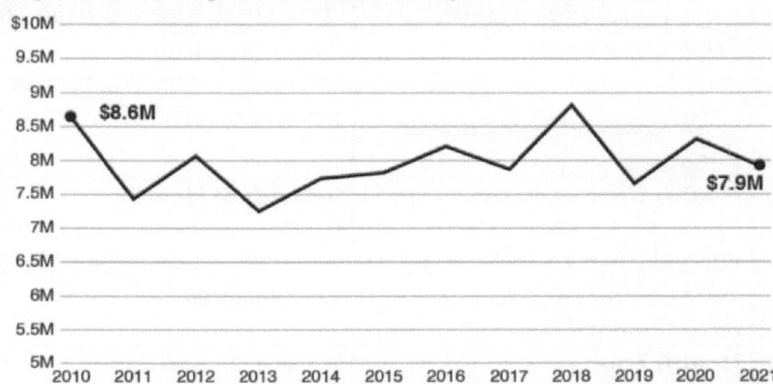

CDC funding from 2010 through 2021 in thousands, adjusted for inflation

Figure 24.2   U.S. Centers for Disease Control and Prevention (CDC) Program Funding Has Declined Since 2010.

Source: This figure was adapted from Matt McKillop and Dara Alpert Lieberman, "The impact of Chronic Underfunding on America's Public Health System: Trends, Risks, and Recommendations" (Washington: Trust for American's Health 2021), available at https://www.tfah.org/report-details/ pandemic-proved-underinvesting-in-public-health-lives-livelihoods-risk/; U.S. Centers for Disease Control and Prevention, "Operating Plans," available at https://www.cdc.gov/budget/operating-plans/index.html (last accessed May 2022); U.S. Bureau of Labor Statistics, "CPI Inflation Calculator," available at https://www. datd.bls.gov/cgi-bin/cpicalc.pl (last accessed May 2022).

Population health is different from the current health system in the following ways (Figure 24.3):

So how is population health different than public health?

Unlike the broad scope of public health, population health zeroes in on targeted interventions tailored to specific communities or population groups. Public health aims to provide maximum benefit for the largest number of people. Population health instead focuses on the health status and health outcomes within a specific group of people.

Population Health	U.S. Health care System Today
Preventive Care: Emphasizes prevention over treatment.	**Reactive Care:** Emphasizes treatment after illness or injury.
Health Determinants: Focuses on factors that influence health, including social, economic and environmental factors.	**Individual Health:** Focuses on treating individuals rather than addressing health determinants.
Health Equity: Aims to reduce health disparities by addressing Social Determinant of Health	**Health Disparities:** Perpetuates health disparities based on socioeconomic status, race and access.

Figure 24.3   Caption: Characteristics of Population Health

Tech-driven *"Health Care Anywhere"*

Connected health consumers are the new norm. They increasingly expect personalized, device-enabled services that are smart and convenient. Health consumers of all ages will benchmark their health care experiences against their other digitized daily living experiences.

Consumer demand and new technology-driven options are rapidly erasing historical industry boundaries. Tech-savvy players are entering the health market with new approaches to giving patients and health consumers what they want.

Wearables and on-the-go health monitoring devices empower individuals to take a proactive approach to their health, leading to better health outcomes and improved quality of life. Devices such as smartwatches and fitness trackers monitor heart rate, blood pressure, and oxygen levels, allowing for continuous health monitoring.

Wearables can already detect abnormalities like irregular heartbeats or abnormal blood oxygen levels, prompting early medical intervention.

Devices help in manage chronic conditions by providing real-time data, which can lead to early detection of potential issues.

Using various forms of artificial intelligence, many devices go beyond passive monitoring to include personalized, intelligent "nudges" to help improve health factors and boost wellness.

Telehealth came into public consciousness with the pandemic and demonstrated that, for certain conditions, it can be both effective and convenient in providing services.

Today the expanding capabilities of telehealth include a variety of services, such as virtual doctor visits, remote patient monitoring, mobile health applications, and digital transmission of medical data.

Benefits of telehealth include:

- Providing medical care for people in rural or underserved areas who may have limited access to healthcare facilities.
- Increasing access to health services for people who have difficulty traveling due to age, disability, or chronic conditions.
- Lowering costs by reducing the need for emergency room visits, hospital admissions, and transportation expenses.

Hospital at Home (HaH) programs enable patients to receive hospital-level care in the comfort of their homes if they need acute care for any of 60 conditions.[9]

It's an approach that has flourished in countries with single-payer health systems, but its use in the US has been limited until now.

For certain medical conditions, HaH provides well-monitored, at-home treatments that are safer, cheaper, and more effective than traditional hospital care.[10]

Johns Hopkins Medicine (Johns Hopkins), in Baltimore, Maryland, has operated a Hospital at Home program since 1994. Their results show that the total cost of at-home care is 32% less than traditional hospital care. The approach also reduced treatment times by one-third. In the end, patient and family satisfaction was higher in the home setting with no differences in the subsequent use of medical services or readmissions.[11]

Universal Coverage

Universal health coverage (UHC) is about ensuring that everyone, regardless of circumstance, can access a baseline of quality health services they need—when and where they need them—without the fear of financial ruin. It's not just about treating illness; it's about a full spectrum of care, from promoting health and preventing disease to offering treatment, rehabilitation, and even palliative care throughout one's life.

Protecting people from the devastating financial burden of paying for health care out of their own pockets is essential. The alternative is a cruel choice—depleting life savings, selling assets, or taking on debt just to afford necessary care. These decisions don't just erode individual futures; they often shatter the prospects of entire families, trapping future generations in cycles of poverty.

Greater Focus on Primary Care

If we want to make a meaningful difference in the health of Americans, we need to look no further than primary care. It's the entry point into the health care system.

Primary care is the basic, first-level health care provided by a medical professional, such as a family doctor, or nurse practitioner who addresses a broad range of health issues, including prevention, diagnosis, treatment, and ongoing management of common medical conditions. It serves as the consumer's initial point of contact with the health care system and focuses on overall health and wellness.

It's the place where comprehensive, accessible, and continuous care begins. By investing more in primary care, we can unlock a cascade of benefits that touch every corner of the system.

Start with access. Primary care providers (PCPs) are on the front lines of disease detection and prevention. They're the ones conducting regular check-ups, screenings, and providing preventive services—identifying health problems before they spiral into something serious. When individuals build a long-term relationship with a PCP, they get consistency. They get coordination. And they get better outcomes. That continuity is the key to more accurate diagnoses and more effective treatment plans, over time.

Next, consider the role of primary care in managing chronic diseases. Diabetes, hypertension, asthma—these are the conditions that, when poorly managed, can dominate lives and drain resources. But with regular monitoring and personalized care plans, primary care can turn the tide. PCPs don't just treat symptoms; they educate. They empower patients with lifestyle changes and self-management techniques, leading to better adherence to treatment plans and, ultimately, better health outcomes.

And then, there's the financial argument. Primary care is far less expensive than the alternatives—specialty care, emergency room visits, or hospitalizations. By addressing health issues early, primary care doesn't just improve health; it lowers costs. Managing chronic conditions effectively means fewer trips to the hospital, fewer ER visits, and fewer costly interventions down the road.

Let's not forget the equity factor. Focusing on primary care brings health care within reach of underserved and marginalized populations. Community health centers and primary care clinics serve as lifelines to those who might otherwise slip through the cracks. And PCPs often go beyond medicine—they address the social determinants of health, from housing and nutrition to employment, that are deeply intertwined with well-being.

When you look globally, the evidence is clear: countries with strong primary care systems have better overall health outcomes—lower mortality rates, and higher life expectancy. Why? Because primary care is holistic. It looks at the whole person—their physical health, their mental health, and their social environment—and crafts personalized, comprehensive treatment plans that get results.

And finally, there's the human element. The trust that builds over time between a patient and their PCP fosters better communication, better adherence to medical advice, and a deeper engagement with their own health. Primary care is, at its core, patient-centered. It's about the individual—about meeting their needs and respecting their preferences. And when people feel heard, respected, and cared for, satisfaction goes up. It's a health care experience they're not just willing to engage with—they're eager to.

In the end, stronger primary care isn't just an investment in the system—it's an investment in people, in their health, and in their lives.

Upstream Social Services

Investing in upstream social services may hold the key to improving health and reducing costs in ways we're only beginning to understand. The data is starting to tell us something important: America's sky-high health care costs aren't just a result of what we spend on medicine, but rather what we don't spend on everything else. Education, housing, nutrition—these are the areas where our reluctance to invest has left us paying a steep price in health care.

Take Humana Health, for example. In Louisville, Kentucky, and four other Southern cities, they've been running a program that provides healthier food to vulnerable communities. The results are hard to ignore—an average of $15 less in monthly health care costs per patient. It's a small number with huge implications. The concept is simple: "Food as Medicine." Give people better nutrition, and you don't just reduce immediate health care costs—you prevent long-term, expensive conditions like diabetes, heart disease, and obesity before they become chronic burdens. [12]

Meanwhile, in Salt Lake City, Intermountain Health is taking this concept even further. They've created an impact investing program designed to fund "upstream" services. These are initiatives that tackle the social factors affecting health like housing stability, employment, and financial wellness. But Intermountain isn't just theorizing; they're acting, basing their efforts on deep research into Utah's specific needs and health assessments from the communities they serve.

And the evidence is clear. Communities that invest in such upstream services see improved health outcomes, lower medical spending, and a reduction in health disparities. When we invest in people's lives—whether that's providing stable housing or supporting financial health—we invest in their well-being, and the entire health care system benefits as a result.

Now Is the Time for Change

Now, more than ever is the time for change. The models explored in this chapter are starting points. These ideas and initiatives are part of a broader tapestry, one that weaves together different programs and strategies to move us toward a healthier, more affordable future.

The path forward in changing the system will require the courage to act. It will take creativity and a willingness to embrace new ways of thinking. Policymakers, health care providers, and citizens must unite to support new innovative health care models.

Such change isn't just about cutting costs. It's about building a system that prioritizes health and well-being for everyone. If you're ready for change, turn the page. Let's take a closer look at what we're up against, and how we can turn things around.

For Your Consideration:

1. How does the current "break-fix" health care model contribute to inefficiencies in the system, and how might value-based care, as described in this chapter, shift the focus to long-term health outcomes?
2. What role does public health investment play in improving overall health and reducing health care costs?
3. Why do you think public health spending is declining despite its proven benefits?
4. How might a shift toward population health and addressing social determinants of health improve equity and outcomes in the health care system?
5. What is the importance of investing in upstream social services like housing, education, and nutrition to improve public health, and how do these investments ultimately impact health care costs?

Notes:

_____

_____

_____

_____

_____

_____

_____

_____

_____

_____

_____

_____

_____

Endnotes

1. Value-Based Care: What It Is, and Why It's Needed, Commonwealth Fund, February 7, 2023, https://www.common-wealthfund.org/publications/explainer/2023/feb/value-based-care-what-it-is-why-its-needed
2. Anne M. Lockner, Insight: The Health care Industry's Shift from Fee-for-Service to Value-Based Reimbursement, Bloomberg Law, September 28, 2016, https://news.bloomberglaw.com/health-law-and-business/insight-the-healthcare-industrys-shift-from-fee-for-service-to-value-based-reimbursement
3. Timothy Tyler Brown, How Effective are Public Health Departments at Preventing Mortality? *Economics & Human Biology*, 13, 2014, 34–45.
4. Timothy Tyler Brown, Returns on Investment in California County Departments of Public Health. *American Journal of Public Health*, 106(8), 2016, 1477–1482.
5. Betty Bekemeier, Youngran Yang, Matthew D. Dunbar, Athena Pantazis, and David E. Grembowski, Targeted health department expenditures benefit birth outcomes at the county level. *American Journal of Preventive Medicine*, 46(6), 2014, 569–577.
6. Betty Bekemeier, David Grembowski, Young Ran Yang, and Jerald R. Herting. Local Public Health Delivery of Maternal Child Health Services: Are Specific Activities Associated with Reductions in Black–White Mortality Disparities? *Maternal and Child Health Journal*, 16(3), 2012, 615–623.
7. Fact Sheet: How Investing in Public Health Will Strengthen America's Health, Center for American Progress, May 17, 2022, https://www.americanprogress.org/article/fact-sheet-how-investing-in-public-health-will-strengthen-americas-health/
8. Social Determinants of Health, World Health Organization, https://www.who.int/health-topics/social-determinants-of-health#tab=tab_1
9. Richard Eisenberg, What to Know About Medicare and Hospital at Home Programs. *Fortune Well*, June 24, 2024, https://fortune.com/well/article/medicare-hospital-at-home-programs/
10. Bruce Leff, Lynda Burton, Scott L. Mader, Bruce Naughton, Jeffrey Burl, Sharon K. Inouye, William B. Greenough III et al., Hospital at Home: Feasibility and Outcomes of a Program

to Provide Hospital-Level Care at Home for Acutely Ill Older Patients. *Annals of Internal Medicine*, 143(11), December 2005, 798–808.

11. Bruce Leff, Lynda Burton, Scott L. Mader, Bruce Naughton, Jeffrey Burl, Sharon K. Inouye, William B. Greenough III et al., Hospital at Home: Feasibility and Outcomes of a Program to Provide Hospital-Level Care at Home for Acutely Ill Older Patients. *Annals of Internal Medicine*, 143(11), December 2005, 798–808.

12. David H. Freedman, Health Care's 'Upstream' Conundrum. *Politico*, January 10, 2018, https://www.politico.com/agenda/ story/2018/01/10/long-term-health-nation-problems-000613/

Chapter 25

From Aspiration to Action

"I was waiting for something extraordinary to happen but as the years wasted on nothing ever did unless I caused it."

—Charles Bukowski

If you've gotten this far in the book, you are now armed with more insights than most Americans as to why the health care system is broken, and maybe even on par with those who run or regulate it. The challenges are significant. The obstacles are real.

The first step in making health care better is the hardest: finding the courage to act. Change doesn't come easily, but it starts with deciding to do something—anything. Small actions, when taken, have the power to spark transformation.

When you advocate for change, you'll often hear, *"It can't be done."* But don't stop there. Dig deeper. Often, *"It can't be done"* really means *"I'm afraid of change"* or *"I don't know how to do it."* That's where the real opportunity for advocacy and transformation begins.

DOI: 10.4324/9781003600695-28

To believe that change is impossible is to accept being on the wrong side of history. The health care system won't fix itself. Left unchecked, it will only get worse.

Here's the good news: we already know that America can afford a world-class health care system. The resources are there; we're just not using them wisely.

Consider this: we spend $4.7 trillion on health care. Ninety-seven percent goes toward treating diseases rather than preventing them. If the health care system was a corporation, its leaders would be fired for its poor return on investment.

Today's system burdens American workers. The rising costs of health care strip us of resources that could otherwise go toward a downpayment on a home, education, or retirement. And businesses? They're struggling to cover skyrocketing benefits while cutting back on new hires.

Up until now most of our elected and health care leaders have focused the health reform debate on changing policies to make the system more efficient.

There are plenty of experts and health care leaders that point fingers and blame someone for the fix we're in. The results we get from this approach are the same as squeezing a balloon. You grab hold in one place thinking you are solving a problem, but another problem pops up somewhere else as a result.

We're at a tipping point. Health care in America will go in one of two ways: we either accept the status quo and prepare for the consequences, or we come together to create a movement that redefines health, well-being, and prosperity of future generations.

Throughout history, we've seen how small changes can ignite profound transformations—women's suffrage, the civil rights movement, marriage equality. Now, it's health care's turn. The question isn't if we can afford to change but rather how much longer we can afford not to.

Even incremental changes would matter. For example, after America, Switzerland is in second place for spending more money per capita than other countries. They spend 12% of their GDP on health care, but their health measures are significantly better. On average, Swiss citizens live six years longer than Americans.

If we could reduce our health care spending to Swiss levels, we'd free up a trillion dollars for other pressing needs.[1] This is a simple example of the real cost of a dysfunctional system. It's also an example of the opportunity we have to redirect resources toward a system that produces better health for all.

Overcoming Inertia

Changing the system starts by changing the narrative. It's not about blaming those in charge but about reimagining the system we're all trapped in. The health care industry is hardwired for short-term gains. Leaders are rewarded for staying focused on immediate results in their narrow part of the system. Insurance companies are incentivized to minimize costs, sometimes by delaying or denying care. Hospitals and doctors' profit from delivering more services, even when the long-term benefits aren't there.

Policymakers? They face the *"long pocket"* problem. The costs of doing the right thing appear immediately, while the benefits may take years to materialize. In the world of short election cycles, that's a hard sell. But it's time to change the conversation, from *"what have you done for me lately"* to *"when are you going to do the right thing?"*

Today, there's a growing chorus of economists, public health experts, and policymakers who are pushing for upstream change—addressing the social determinants of health instead of playing an expensive game of catch-up.

We have the knowledge, the technology, and the expertise to create a health care system that's equitable, efficient, and effective.

This is where activism comes in. When we rally for changing health care, we amplify the voices of the marginalized. We hold leaders accountable. We drive policy changes that begin to transform the system.

Just like civil rights, women's suffrage, and marriage equality, health care reform is a cause worth fighting for. The stakes are high: universal access, preventive care, economic stability, and improved quality of life for every American.

So, what can you do? Educate yourself. Advocate for change. Join or support advocacy groups. Vote for candidates who prioritize positive changes that move us in the direction of improving health.

The path to change won't be easy. But together, through collective action, we have the power to transform health care in America and build a system that ensures health, well-being, and opportunity for all. Now is the time to act. Now is the time to shape the future of health care for generations to come.

For Your Consideration:

1. What are the issues that are most important to you when it comes to making changes to improve the current health care system?
2. What small actions or steps can individuals take to begin advocating for meaningful health care reform, and why is it often difficult to get started?
3. The chapter compares health care reform to other transformative movements like civil rights and women's rights. Do you agree with this comparison? If yes, in what ways can activism for health care follow similar paths to drive change?
4. Is changing health care important enough for you to take some type of action that leads to change? If yes, what are one or two things you can see yourself doing?

Notes:

_____

_____

_____

_____

_____

_____

_____

_____

_____

_____

_____

_____

_____

Endnote

1. Der Spiegel, What's Wrong With America?: "The Despair Is Smoldering in Society," June 24, 2020.

Chapter 26

The Future Is Not What It Used to Be

"It always seems impossible until it is done"

—Nelson Mandela

It's 2035 and a most remarkable year is coming to a close. A populus-driven movement, which began in earnest in the previous decade, has swept the country. Bold ideas and new investments that have been supported by enlightened elected officials, committed clinicians, savvy business leaders, and consumers are bearing fruit.

A health and economic revolution has unmistakably taken hold.

America has become a healthier, more equitable nation. A transformation in how we create health and provide health care has fundamentally altered the nation's societal fabric.

Hard fought battles to change an unjust and broken system have leveled the playing field. Everyone now has the *opportunity* to live healthier lives.

Central to the change that has occurred is a proactive approach to health. Preventive care is now a fundamental

   DOI: 10.4324/9781003600695-29

component of the health care system. Regular screenings, vaccinations, and wellness programs are universally available and
encouraged.

This shift has led to dramatic declines in chronic diseases.
Diabetes, hypertension, and heart disease are caught early and
managed effectively. Public health campaigns have fostered
a culture of wellness, where exercise and balanced diets are
prioritized and celebrated.

Families are no longer forced to choose between health
care and basic necessities. Individuals no longer avoid seeking
care because they are underinsured or can't afford it.

Health equity has become more than a slogan or aspiration.
Communities that once faced systemic disadvantages now benefit from targeted interventions designed to uplift and holistically support their well-being.

Recognizing that health is influenced by many factors
outside of clinical settings, elected and business leaders have
advanced an inter-related set of laws and policies that improve
housing, education, and nutrition. Initiatives to reduce poverty
and improve living conditions have had a profound impact on
public health measures.

Mental health is treated with the same urgency and importance as physical health. This all-encompassing approach to
well-being raises the bar for pursuing happiness and self-
actualization. It goes beyond merely reducing the presence
of harmful and debilitating conditions that previously limited
citizens from achieving their true and unique potential.

Freed from the shackles of the past, clinicians, researchers,
and public health experts are swept up in a health and medical renaissance.

Health practitioners at all stages of their careers are freed
to restore themselves and bring more humanity back into the
practice of caring for others.

The financial incentives of the past have been upended.
Doctors, hospitals, and other health practitioners are rewarded

for measurably improving the health of individuals and populations in their care. When interventional services are needed, they are readily available, accessible, and high quality.

The best and brightest students from all walks of life set their sights on careers that allow them to apply their talents and make a difference.

Technological advancements have played a pivotal role in this transformation. Telehealth, once a novelty, has become an integral part of our health care delivery system. Patients in rural areas or those with mobility issues now have seamless access to medical professionals, breaking down geographic barriers.

Wearable health devices and mobile apps continuously monitor vital signs and health metrics, providing real-time data to both patients and providers. This integration of technology has empowered individuals to take control of their health, fostering a sense of agency and accountability.

The economy? Thriving, of course. A healthy populace is a productive populace. Companies have figured out that unhealthy workers and bloated insurance premiums are bad for business. Workplace wellness is seamlessly tied to other components of a system. The work-life balance among American workers has been recalibrated.

Health as a percentage of GDP drops as the output from investing in health produces measurable health dividends. This turbocharges the innovation of American-based companies which climb higher in the global markets. As this happens economic dividends accrue to both shareholders and workers.

Sound like a dream? Maybe. But as you close your eyes at the end of this day think about the world you want to live in and the legacy you want to create for your children and others yet to come onto this planet.

We can do better. It won't be easy, but it can be done.

And it all starts with *you.*

For Your Consideration:

1. What are the most important things you learned from reading this book?
2. What are the most important things you believe need to change?
3. Do you feel more empowered to take actions that make a difference? Why or why not?
4. What first step are you willing to take to make your views known to others? What micro-actions might you take in the next 30 days?

Notes:

_____
_____
_____
_____
_____
_____
_____
_____
_____
_____
_____
_____
_____
_____
_____
_____
_____

Continue Your Journey

Scan This QR Code or go to www.healthcarenation.us for news
and additional resources.

Scan me!

Index

Note: *Italic* page numbers refer to figures.

Routledge Focus on Applied Linguistics

For more information about this series, please visit: https://www.routledge.com/Routledge-Focus-on-Applied-Linguistics/book-series/RFAL